Progress Monitoring Assessments

McGraw Hill Education

mheducation.com/prek-12

Copyright © McGraw-Hill Education

Send all inquiries to:
McGraw-Hill Education
Two Penn Plaza
New York, New York 10121

ISBN: 978-0-07-901748-2
MHID: 0-07-901748-7

Printed in the United States of America.

6 7 8 9 LOV 23 22 21   A

Table of Contents

Progress Monitoring Assessments

The *Progress Monitoring Assessments* component is an integral part of the complete assessment program aligned with *Wonders.*

Purpose

Consistent use of these assessments allows you to monitor your students' progress through the curriculum in a steady and structured manner. When used as formative assessments, the test results provide data you can use to inform subsequent instruction.

Focus

As students complete each genre study in *Wonders*, they are assessed on their understanding of the key comprehension skills and vocabulary strategies they have studied. These items measure students' ability to access meaning from texts and demonstrate their understanding of unknown and multiple-meaning words and phrases.

Overview

Assessments follow the genre-based focus of *Wonders*. The structure and format of the tests is the same in every unit. *Genre Study 1 (Weeks 1 and 2)* and *Genre Study 2 (Weeks 3 and 4)* tests include two short selections, each with two associated items assessing either comprehension skills or vocabulary strategies, and one longer selection with six associated items assessing both comprehension and vocabulary. *Genre Study 3 (Week 5)* tests reflect the shorter period of instruction and include one selection with five associated items assessing both comprehension and vocabulary.

Just as *Wonders* encompasses the flexibility to teach the elements of the program in your own way, the *Progress Monitoring Assessments* allow you to test in your own way, too. Sometimes you may want to use the brief comprehension and/or vocabulary portions of a two-week assessment as a quick check of how students are responding after the first week of instruction, saving the remaining portion of the assessment for the conclusion of instruction. At other times, you may prefer to administer the entire ten-item assessment at one sitting, at the conclusion of the genre study instruction.

Reading Selections

To support the focus of classroom instruction, the reading selections reflect unit themes and Essential Questions. Every reading selection is a "cold," or new, read. This allows students to apply what they have learned and allows you to evaluate the degree of mastery they have achieved.

Each progress monitoring assessment for *Genre Studies 1 and 2* features two short selections and one longer selection; each *Genre Study 3* assessment features one informational text or poem. Selections increase in complexity as the school year progresses to mirror the rigor of reading materials students encounter in the classroom. The Lexile® goal by unit is as follows:

- Unit 1: 520L
- Unit 2: 580L
- Unit 3: 640L
- Unit 4: 700L
- Unit 5: 760L
- Unit 6: 820L

Assessment Items

Each assessment for *Genre Studies 1 and 2* features nine multiple-choice items and one technology-enhanced item, while each *Genre Study 3* one-week assessment includes four multiple-choice items and one technology-enhanced item. (Please note that the print versions of technology-enhanced items are available in this component; the full functionality of the items is available only through the online assessment center.) This variety of item types provides different ways to assess student understanding, allows for deeper investigation into skills and strategies, and provides students an opportunity to become familiar with the kinds of items they may encounter in state-mandated assessments.

Administering
Progress Monitoring Assessments

Make copies of the assessment for the class. You will need one copy of the answer key page for each student.

After each student has a copy of the assessment, provide a version of the following directions: **Say:** *Write your name on the question pages for this assessment.* (When students are finished, continue with the directions.) *You will read selections and answer questions about them. Read each selection and the questions that follow it carefully. For the multiple-choice questions, circle the letter next to the correct answer. For the question that asks you to write on the page, you may be asked to match, circle, or underline choices, complete a chart, or place details in order. Look carefully at the directions before you write your answer. When you have completed the assessment, put your pencil down and turn the pages over. You may begin now.*

Answer procedural questions during the assessment, but do not provide any assistance on the items or selections. After the class has completed the assessment, ask students to verify that their names are written on the necessary pages.

Scoring

Use the scoring chart at the bottom of the answer key to record each student's score. Test items are worth two points each. Technology-enhanced items should be answered correctly in full, although you may choose to provide partial credit. Each complete *Genre Study 1 and 2* assessment totals 20 points, while each *Genre Study 3* assessment totals 10 points, for a total of 50 points per unit.

Along with the correct answers and the content focus of the test items, the answer keys provide item complexity (measured by Depth of Knowledge, or DOK) information. For additional scoring assistance, rationales are provided for every assessment item. These rationales explain why the correct answer choice meets the full expectations of the item and why the distractors are lacking this attribute.

Further metadata is available in the online assessment center. The accumulated data from the assessments provides a picture of your students' progress.

Evaluating Scores

Use the assessment results in conjunction with your personal observations to gather the formative information you need to better understand your students' performance and help guide your decisions about individualized instructional and intervention needs.

The expectation is for students to score 80% or higher on each assessment. For students who do not meet this benchmark, assign appropriate lessons from the relevant **Tier 2 online PDFs**. Refer to the Progress Monitoring pages that follow each genre study in the Teacher's Editions of *Wonders* for specific lessons.

Information gathered by evaluating the results of these tests also can be used to diagnose your students' specific strengths and weaknesses. If you use *Progress Monitoring Assessments* scores to help determine report card grades, then you can consider the tests to be summative assessments as well.

This column lists the instructional content for the genre study that is assessed in each item.

Question	Correct Answer	Content Focus	Complexity

This column lists the Depth of Knowledge associated with each item.

Question	Correct Answer	Content Focus	Complexity
5	B	Main Idea and Key Details	DOK 2
6	C	Context Clues	DOK 2

Scoring rows identify items associated with the assessed skills and allow for quick record keeping.

Comprehension 1, 2, 5, 7, 10	/10	%
Vocabulary 3, 4, 6, 8, 9	/10	%
Total Progress Monitoring Assessment Score	/20	%

Read the passage. Then answer the questions.

The Clay Storyteller

Vwomp, the wheels of a car scrape. The car contains a load of cedar from almost 100 miles away. The cedar is for Helen Cordero. She needs the wood for her fire.

Cordero is a potter, like her grandfather, whom she loved. She brings new life to pottery. Cordero does not use a potter's wheel. Instead, she begins by hand-shaping the pottery using the rich soil of New Mexico.

Cordero has decided to create figures, but not the usual birds or animals. She has found a way to honor her grandfather, his pottery, and his stories. She is creating a storyteller doll of her grandfather. Until now, no one has made a storyteller like this one. It is Cordero's own invention.

First, Cordero shapes her grandfather. Then, she adds five grandchildren climbing on him to listen. It is a scene of children taught by adults. She holds the clay figure over an open fire. Cordero likes using the old ways. Later, she paints the figure at her kitchen table.

Other artists take notice of Cordero's work. They begin making storyteller figures. The storyteller figures become popular, as does Cordero and her village. Everybody who collects the figures sees a special story in them.

GO ON →

1 Read the paragraph from the passage.

First, Cordero shapes her grandfather. Then, she adds five grandchildren climbing on him to listen. It is a scene of children taught by adults. She holds the clay figure over an open fire. Cordero likes using the old ways. Later, she paints the figure at her kitchen table.

What does the paragraph help readers understand?

A why Cordero uses a potter's wheel

B what animals Cordero models her art after

C how Cordero creates her clay figures

D when Cordero became an artist

2 Read the diagram.

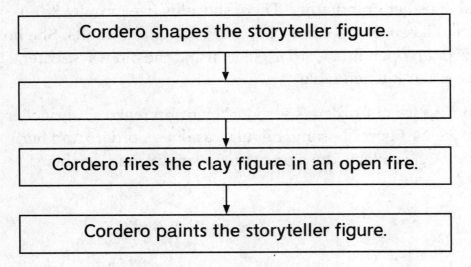

| Cordero shapes the storyteller figure. |
| Cordero fires the clay figure in an open fire. |
| Cordero paints the storyteller figure. |

Which sentence best completes the order in the diagram?

A Cordero wants to honor her grandfather.

B Cordero adds grandchildren climbing on their grandfather.

C Other artists get famous for making storyteller figures too.

D The car arrives with cedar wood for the fire.

GO ON →

Read the passage. Then answer the questions.

Joyful Lion Dancing

Bam, Clang, GONG! The sound of traditional Chinese music floats through the air. People in the school follow it to see what is happening. What they find is a giant lion dancing for them!

The lion is not real. It is a big puppet that has dancers inside of it. Yang Ho is one of those dancers. He walks around with a lion's head on that is made of paper and fur. The head is part of a larger costume. Ho and his fellow students make up the lion. Together, they perform the lion dance for the people that have gathered.

But putting on the dance is no easy task. Dancers must practice the footsteps needed to follow the beat of drums and gongs. In the past, movements would show power. They made the lion look dangerous. Now, modern moves are more playful. Ho likes putting the two dance styles together.

Today, the Lion Dance Troupe performs to start the new school year. The dancer inside the lion's tail helps the giant puppet stand. *Bam* goes the drums, and *clang, gong* sings the music. The crowd of students cheers loudly.

GO ON →

3   Read the sentence from the passage.

It is a big puppet that has dancers inside of it.

Which word from the sentence is a compound word?

A big

B puppet

C dancers

D inside

4   Read the sentence from the passage.

Dancers must practice the <u>footsteps</u> needed to follow the beat of drums and gongs.

What does the word <u>footsteps</u> show about the dancers?

A how they sing along

B how they clap their hands

C how they move their feet

D how they spin around

GO ON →

Read the passage. Then answer the questions.

The First (Not-So-) Blue Jeans

Jacob Davis was facing the challenge of a lifetime. A customer had just left his tailor shop in Reno, Nevada. She had posed an interesting problem to him. The woman needed Davis to make her husband special pants. They needed to be extra durable. They couldn't fall apart. Her husband's current work pants, she explained, ripped and tore far too easily.

Davis knew he could solve the problem. He was trained to be a tailor in his hometown of Riga, Latvia. This was where he was born in 1831 and raised by Jewish parents. In 1854, he came to America to practice his trade. He could use what he knew to help this woman.

Davis thought about the materials he used every day in his shop. The fabric was the first place to start. He looked closely at his stock of cotton fabric and focused on two: duck cloth and denim. He ordered both from a company in San Francisco, California. It was called Levi Strauss and Company. Both fabrics were made from tightly-knitted cotton. The only difference was in how the threads were woven. Davis decided to work with sturdy duck cloth.

Next, he thought about sewing the pants. How could he make the seams stronger? He looked at the supplies he used in his shop. Davis made items besides clothes. For example, he sold tents and covers for wagons. Then he thought about his horse blankets. Sometimes, Davis used metal fasteners. These fasteners were called rivets. That's it! Davis added copper rivets to the corners of the pants. They helped to keep the fabric from coming apart.

Davis' idea was a success! Not only did the pants work, but people began to hear about how durable they were. Soon, they also asked to buy his pants. Other tailors copied Davis' work. He knew that he must protect his idea. To do so, he had to apply for a patent from the government. But Davis could not afford the fee. For help, he turned to the man who supplied his fabric. After all, Davis would need a lot of duck cloth for his new pants!

GO ON →

Davis wrote Levi Strauss a letter. He tried to explain why his pants were special. "The secret of them Pents," he wrote, "is the Rivits that I put in those Pockets and I found the demand so large that I cannot make them up fast enough." Davis explained that he was selling his pants for three dollars apiece. This was a high price for pants at this time.

Strauss agreed that the pants were special. He hoped to sell them to the hard-working miners in San Francisco. Strauss asked Davis to move to San Francisco. He wanted the two men to become business partners.

Before long, Davis and his family left Reno. They moved to San Francisco. Davis started working at Levi Strauss and Company. He continued to try new ideas for clothing. Soon, he would build new pants using blue denim. This fabric was strong. But it stretched better than the duck cloth. And today's popular blue jeans were born!

GO ON →

5 Read the sentences from the passage.

Jacob Davis was facing the challenge of a lifetime. A customer had just left his tailor shop in Reno, Nevada.

Which word from the sentences is a compound word?

    A challenge

    B lifetime

    C customer

    D tailor

6 What did Davis have to do before he could begin sewing the pants?

    A apply for a patent from the government

    B order the fabric he would use

    C add rivets to the corners of the pants

    D move to San Francisco

7 What happened after Davis was able to make durable work pants?

    A More people started wearing pants.

    B He thought about adding rivets to the pants.

    C People wanted to buy his work pants.

    D He started using duck cloth for his pants.

GO ON →

8   Read the sentence from the passage.

Davis explained that he was selling his pants for three dollars <u>apiece</u>.

What does the compound word <u>apiece</u> mean?

A   all

B   never

C   always

D   each

9   Circle **three** words from the passage that are compound words.

interesting

hometown

difference

sometimes

cannot

partners

continued

GO ON →

Progress Monitoring Assessments

10 How is the information in the passage organized?

A by showing the sequence of events that led to the invention of blue jeans

B by telling the effects of trying different types of fabric for work pants

C by explaining how each solution created a new problem for Davis

D by mentioning other tailors who were also making work pants at the time

Student Name: _____

Question	Correct Answer	Content Focus	Complexity
1	C	Text Structure: Sequence	DOK 2
2	B	Text Structure: Sequence	DOK 2
3	D	Compound Words	DOK 1
4	C	Compound Words	DOK 1
5	B	Compound Words	DOK 1
6	B	Text Structure: Sequence	DOK 2
7	C	Text Structure: Sequence	DOK 2
8	D	Compound Words	DOK 1
9	see below	Compound Words	DOK 1
10	A	Text Structure: Sequence	DOK 3

Comprehension 1, 2, 6, 7, 10	/10	%
Vocabulary 3, 4, 5, 8, 9	/10	%
Total Progress Monitoring Assessment Score	/20	%

9   Students should circle the following words:
- hometown
- sometimes
- cannot

Unit 1 Weeks 1–2 Rationales

1

A is incorrect because the author does not talk about the potter's wheel in this paragraph.

B is incorrect because Cordero doesn't make animal figures.

C is correct because the author describes the procedure that Cordero follows to create her storyteller clay figure.

D is incorrect because the author does not give this information in the entire passage.

2

A is incorrect because this happens before Cordero shapes the storyteller figure.

B is correct because Cordero adds the grandchildren to show they are listening to the storyteller.

C is incorrect because this detail is not part of the sequence of events related to making the storyteller figure.

D is incorrect because the car arrives at the very beginning of the passage.

3

A is incorrect because the word *big* is not a compound word made up of two smaller words.

B is incorrect because the word *puppet* is not a compound word.

C is incorrect because the word *dancers* is not a compound word.

D is correct because the word *inside* is made up of the words *in* and *side*.

4

A is incorrect because the word parts of *footsteps* do not have anything to do with singing.

B is incorrect because the word *footsteps* has to do with feet, not hands.

C is correct because *footsteps* includes the words *foot* and *steps,* suggesting the movement of feet.

D is incorrect because the word parts in *footsteps* do not necessarily have to do with spinning around.

5

A is incorrect because the word *challenge* is not a compound word.

B is correct because the word *lifetime* is made up of the words *life* and *time*.

C is incorrect because the word *customer* is not made up of two smaller words.

D is incorrect because the word *tailor* is not a compound word.

6

A is incorrect because Davis began sewing the pants without having to apply for a patent.

B is correct because Davis needed the right fabric before he could begin sewing the pants.

C is incorrect because Davis added rivets to the pants after having already sewed them.

D is incorrect because Davis moved to San Francisco after he had already created the pants.

7

A is incorrect because the passage does not discuss how many people in general wore pants.

B is incorrect because Davis used rivets when he first created the pants.

C is correct because once people heard that the pants worked, they wanted to have a pair also.

D is incorrect because Davis chose duck cloth at the beginning of the process before he made the pants.

8

A is incorrect because *apiece* includes the words *a* and *piece*, which do not suggest that the compound word means "all."

B is incorrect because the word parts of *apiece* do not indicate that it means "never."

C is incorrect because *apiece* does not have word parts that mean "always."

D is correct because *apiece* includes *a* and *piece*, which suggests that the word means "each."

9

Hometown, *sometimes*, and *cannot* are all compound words.

10

A is correct because the author organizes the information to show how one event leads to another until Davis and Strauss become partners and invent blue jeans.

B is incorrect because the passage tells about trying only one type of fabric for work pants and being successful.

C is incorrect because Davis is able to solve the problem of creating durable work pants; there are no other problems after he finds that solution.

D is incorrect because only at the end does the passage mention how Davis needed to get a patent because others were interested in making the same kind of work pants.

Read the passage. Then answer the questions.

The Yule Book Flood

Jon did not have much money to buy holiday gifts. But he wanted to get his sister, Katrin, something really special. She always gave him exciting presents. He did not want to disappoint her with a gift she would not like. Jon was feeling pretty low.

That evening, Jon's great-uncle came over for dinner. He could see that Jon was upset.

"What's wrong, Jon?" he asked. "Why are you so quiet?"

"I'm embarrassed. I didn't save enough money to buy Katrin a good gift," replied Jon.

Jon's great-uncle thought for a minute. Then he began to tell Jon a story. When he was little, times were hard. His country, Iceland, was involved in a great war. Stores did not have fancy holiday gifts to sell. But people could afford to buy books. Instead of letting hardships ruin the holidays, the people of Iceland began a new tradition of giving books as gifts.

"This tradition, called the Yule Book Flood, continues today," he said. "Perhaps Katrin would enjoy a special book from you."

"That's a great idea! We can keep your tradition alive here in America," exclaimed Jon.

GO ON →

1   When does Jon's great-uncle begin to tell him his story?

    A   before a great war happened in the country of Iceland

    B   before he knows that Jon did not save enough of his chore money

    C   after Jon tells him that he likes the idea of buying his sister a book

    D   after he finds out that Jon does not have money to buy his sister a gift

2   What happens at the end of the passage?

    A   Jon feels embarrassed.

    B   Jon spends the money he earned.

    C   Jon decides to give his sister a book.

    D   Jon listens to a story.

GO ON →

Read the passage. Then answer the questions.

Color and Joy

Grandma Lopez was spending the afternoon with me until my parents came home. She wanted me to know about things she did when she was growing up in Mexico.

"Taryn, I'm going to teach you to make flowers," said Grandma Lopez.

"I know how to plant flowers," I replied.

"No," she laughed. "We are constructing flowers from paper."

"Why?" I asked.

"I made paper flowers in Mexico. We made them together as a family during a special holiday. Ours were always large," she said.

She explained that the holiday is a time for remembering family members. "It's not a gloomy time, but rather it is like a two-day party."

As we folded yellow tissue paper into flowers, Grandma Lopez told me more about the holiday. "The party is full of color and joy. People sing and dance as a way to honor their loved ones."

"I like this holiday!" I said. Then I fanned out my paper flowers. I imagined that they had a sweet smell, just like the flowers Grandma Lopez had described. I could see how our sunny yellow flowers could make people smile!

GO ON →

3 Read the sentence from the passage.

"We are <u>constructing</u> flowers from paper."

What does the word <u>constructing</u> mean?

A thinking

B holding

C making

D stopping

4 Read the sentence from the passage.

"It's not a <u>gloomy</u> time, but rather it is like a two-day party."

What does the word <u>gloomy</u> mean?

A very sad

B not usual

C easy

D simple

GO ON →

Read the passage. Then answer the questions.

The Ship of the Desert

Uzma waited with her father in line. They were still far away from the front. She leaned to the side to get a better view of the camels. They looked so large, and she wondered if it would be scary to sit on the hump of one. Uzma felt like she should know more about camels. They were a part of her culture.

Suddenly, she thought of something. "Dad, how did camels become so important to our culture?"

Uzma's father looked at the long line in front of them and decided he had time to tell her a story. . .

"Long ago, a man was traveling on the edge of the desert. He carried food and water on his back. The man was returning to his family from far away, but the hot sun and the heavy load he lugged made the journey difficult.

Suddenly, he saw a large, brown creature ahead of him. It bellowed at him, and the loud noise frightened him! The man rushed away. He ran as fast as he could, even with his heavy load.

The next day, he came across a similar creature. This time, the creature was at the far end of a small pool of water. It kept drinking and drinking. Curious, the man carefully inched closer to get a better look. The creature had long, skinny legs and a long, thick neck. Most remarkably, it had a huge hump on its back.

The third day, the man saw more and more of these odd creatures. He decided to observe them carefully to see what he could learn. They ate plants and drank water for long periods of time. The creatures, he learned, were actually meek and gentle.

The man watched the creatures coming over a high sand dune. He knew the desert extended for miles and miles past that dune. 'These creatures must be able to walk in the desert without water for a long time!' he thought.

GO ON →

Copyright © McGraw-Hill Education

On the fourth day, the man came across one of the gentle giants. It was down in the sand with its eyes closed, dozing. The man had an idea.

'Perhaps this creature could help me carry my load,' he thought. So he walked quietly up to the animal. He slipped a rope around its mouth and back over its ears. Then he loaded all of his belongings onto the creature's back and slipped onto its hump.

The animal awoke and got to its feet. The man rode it all the way home! His children greeted him excitedly. They too wanted to ride the wonderful creature.

'Now we can make the desert our home!' the man said happily. And that is how the camel came to be humans' great helper. And that is why we call it 'The Ship of the Desert.'"

Uzma laughed at her father's wonderful story. She started to ask a question. However, she stopped when she realized they had made it to the front of the line.

"Did you say something?" asked her father.

"Never mind," said Uzma with a smile. "I'm going to find out in just a minute!"

GO ON →

Progress Monitoring Assessments

5 Read the sentence from the passage.

The man was returning to his family from far away, but the hot sun and the heavy load he <u>lugged</u> made the journey difficult.

What does the word <u>lugged</u> mean?

A   paid for

B   searched for

C   thought about

D   carried along

6 How is the story about the man in the desert organized?

A   to show why the man is walking in the desert in the first place

B   to show how the man gets knowledge about the camels over time

C   to show how the desert compares to other places the man has been

D   to show why the desert is the best place for the man to live

7 Read the sentence from the passage.

He decided to <u>observe</u> them carefully to see what he could learn.

Which word from the sentence helps the reader understand the meaning of <u>observe</u>?

A   decided

B   see

C   could

D   learn

GO ON →

8   Read the sentence from the passage.

It was down in the sand with its eyes closed, <u>dozing</u>.

What does the word <u>dozing</u> mean?

A sleeping

B running

C fighting

D drinking

9   Which sentence from the passage tells what happens after the man rides the creature all the way home?

A "The man rushed away."

B "It kept drinking and drinking."

C "The animal awoke and got to its feet."

D "His children greeted him excitedly."

GO ON →

10 Put the events in the correct order from 1 to 5. Write the correct number in front of **each** event.

_____ The man rides the animal all the way home.

_____ The man walks through the desert to return to his family.

_____ The man sees a creature that scares him.

_____ The man realizes the animals don't need water for a long time.

_____ The man watches the animals and learns about them.

Answer Key

Student Name: _____

Question	Correct Answer	Content Focus	Complexity
1	D	Character, Setting, Plot: Sequence	DOK 2
2	C	Character, Setting, Plot: Sequence	DOK 1
3	C	Context Clues	DOK 2
4	A	Context Clues	DOK 2
5	D	Context Clues	DOK 2
6	B	Character, Setting, Plot: Sequence	DOK 2
7	B	Context Clues	DOK 2
8	A	Context Clues	DOK 2
9	D	Character, Setting, Plot: Sequence	DOK 2
10	see below	Character, Setting, Plot: Sequence	DOK 2

Comprehension 1, 2, 6, 9, 10	/10		%
Vocabulary 3, 4, 5, 7, 8	/10		%
Total Progress Monitoring Assessment Score	/20		%

10 Students should put the events in the following order:
- 1 - The man walks through the desert to return to his family.
- 2 - The man sees a creature that scares him.
- 3 - The man watches the animals and learns about them.
- 4 - The man realizes the animals don't need water for a long time.
- 5 - The man rides the animal all the way home.

Unit 1 Weeks 3–4 Rationales

1

A is incorrect because Jon's great-uncle begins the story after a great war happened in Iceland.

B is incorrect because Jon's great-uncle begins the story after he finds out that Jon did not save enough money.

C is incorrect because Jon's great-uncle begins the story before Jon tells him that he likes the idea of buying a book.

D is correct because Jon's great-uncle begins the story after he finds out that Jon does not have money to buy his sister a gift.

2

A is incorrect because Jon feels embarrassed at the beginning of the passage.

B is incorrect because Jon spent the money he earned before the passage began.

C is correct because Jon decides it's a great idea to give a book at the end of the passage.

D is incorrect because Jon listens to a story in the middle of the passage.

3

A is incorrect because the word *constructing* does not mean "thinking," and there are no clues to support that option.

B is incorrect because the word *constructing* does not mean "holding," and there are no clues to support that option.

C is correct because the word *constructing* means "making," and there are clues to support that option.

D is incorrect because the word *constructing* does not mean "stopping," and there are no clues to support that option.

4

A is correct because the word *gloomy* means "very sad," and there are clues to support that option.

B is incorrect because the word *gloomy* does not mean "not usual," and there are no clues to support that option.

C is incorrect because the word *gloomy* does not mean "easy," and there are no clues to support that option.

D is incorrect because the word *gloomy* does not mean "simple," and there are no clues to support that option.

5

A is incorrect because the word *lugged* does not mean the man "paid for" the heavy load.

B is incorrect because the word *lugged* does not mean the man "searched for" the heavy load.

C is incorrect because the word *lugged* does not mean the man "thought about" the heavy load.

D is correct because the word *lugged* means the man "carried along" the heavy load.

6

A is incorrect because the story about the man in the desert does not show why the man is walking in the desert.

B is correct because the story about the man in the desert shows how the man gets more knowledge about the camels over time.

C is incorrect because the story about the man in the desert does not show how the desert compares to other places the man has been.

D is incorrect because the story about the man in the desert does not show why the desert is the best place for the man to live.

7

A is incorrect because "decided" does not help the reader understand the meaning of the word *observe*.

B is correct because "see" helps the reader understand the meaning of the word *observe*.

C is incorrect because "could" does not help the reader understand the meaning of the word *observe*.

D is incorrect because "learn" does not help the reader understand the meaning of the word *observe*.

8

A is correct because the word *dozing* means "sleeping," and there is evidence in the passage to support that.

B is incorrect because the word *dozing* does not mean "running," and there is no evidence in the passage to support that it does.

C is incorrect because the word *dozing* does not mean "fighting," and there is no evidence in the passage to support that it does.

D is incorrect because the word *dozing* does not mean "drinking," and there is no evidence in the passage to support that it does.

9

A is incorrect because this sentence tells what happened after the man first saw the camel.

B is incorrect because this sentence tells what happened after the man saw a camel for the second time.

C is incorrect because this sentence tells what happened after the man first got on the camel.

D is correct because this sentence tells what happened after the man rode the camel home.

10

Students should put the events in the following correct order:
The man walks through the desert to return to his family.
The man sees a creature that scares him.
The man watches the animals and learns about them.
The man realizes the animals don't need water for a long time.
The man rides the animal all the way home.

Read the passage. Then answer the questions.

Protecting the River of Grass

Over the flat land of southern Florida lie ponds, marshes, and forests. Together, they form the Everglades. People used to call the Everglades "the river of grass." Water flowed through the sawgrass marshes. This made the marshes look like a river of grass. But now, the Everglades are in trouble and need help.

The Everglades changed for the worse when the state of Florida began to drain or take away some of the water. This allowed farmers to grow crops. Large farms and then cities sprang up. The draining went on as canals and dams moved water out of the Everglades into the ocean. The river of grass was no longer a river.

These changes continue to this day and must be stopped. The government needs to do more to protect the Everglades. Animals that have lived there for hundreds of years are in danger. Plants that had once grown in the Everglades cannot live there now. New plants have taken over. Salty water has moved into the marshes. Many of the alligators have died. The Everglades is half the size it was a hundred years ago! What is left of the Everglades is still in a lot of trouble.

One way to save the Everglades is to stop the dirty water from farms and cities that runs into Lake Okeechobee. Much of the Everglades' water comes from the lake. There need to be more laws to stop the pollution from these fields. Otherwise the dirty water will keep spreading, and the rest of the Everglades will continue to be in trouble.

Another solution is to catch fresh water that now flows into the ocean and bring the water back to the Everglades. In 2000, Florida and the national government worked out a plan to do just that. But the plan has been taking a long time, and many people have worked to stop the effort.

GO ON →

It's hard not to be moved by the landscape of the Everglades. Protecting the beauty of the Everglades is very important. People need to see the Everglades as the amazing place it is. The focus should be on keeping the water of the Everglades clean and having the rare plants and animals there. The Everglades should be a treasure for everyone and stay a place of wonder.

GO ON →

Progress Monitoring Assessments

1   Which sentence **best** states the main idea of the passage?

   A "This allowed farmers to grow crops."

   B "The government needs to do more to protect the Everglades."

   C "Animals that have lived there for hundreds of years are in danger."

   D "In 2000, Florida and the national government worked out a plan to do just that."

2   Where does the name "the river of grass" come from?

   A Florida having ponds, marshes, and forests

   B the Everglades being in trouble

   C water flowing through the sawgrass marshes

   D salty water moving into the marshes

3   Read the sentence from the passage.

   Otherwise the dirty water will keep spreading, and the <u>rest</u> of the Everglades will continue to be in trouble.

   Which meaning of the word <u>rest</u> is used in the sentence?

   A the act of sleeping

   B a break from exercise

   C a place to stop

   D the part that is left over

GO ON →

4   Read the sentence from the passage.

It's hard not to be <u>moved</u> by the landscape of the Everglades.

What does the word <u>moved</u> mean?

A   changed from one position to another

B   to bring out emotions

C   gone from one home to a new home

D   to make a formal request

5   Complete the diagram with the phrases from the box below. Write the main idea in the rectangle. Write the details in the circles.

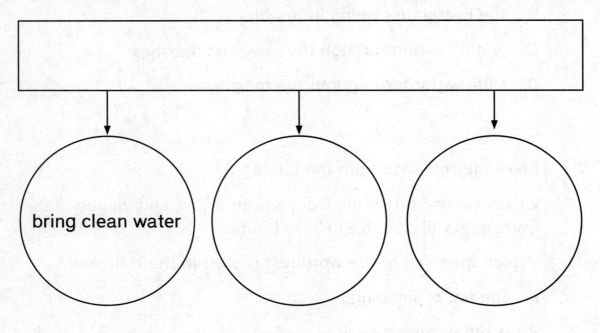

bring clean water

return rare plants and animals

help protect the Everglades

stop the pollution

Question	Correct Answer	Content Focus	Complexity
1	B	Main Idea and Key Details	DOK 2
2	C	Main Idea and Key Details	DOK 2
3	D	Multiple-Meaning Words	DOK 2
4	B	Multiple-Meaning Words	DOK 2
5	see below	Main Idea and Key Details	DOK 2

Comprehension 1, 2, 5		/6	%
Vocabulary 3, 4		/4	%
Total Progress Monitoring Assessment Score		/10	%

5 Students should write the following in the diagram:
- Main Idea: help protect the Everglades
- Details: return rare plants and animals; stop the pollution

Unit 1 Week 5 Rationales

1

A is incorrect because it is a detail about the Everglades.

B is correct because it tells what the entire passage is mainly about.

C is incorrect because it is a detail about a danger to the Everglades.

D is incorrect because it is a detail about a plan to save the Everglades.

2

A is incorrect because the name does not come from Florida having ponds, marshes, and forests.

B is incorrect because the name does not come from the Everglades being in trouble.

C is correct because water flowing through the sawgrass marshes looks like a river of grass.

D is incorrect because the name does not come from salty water moving into the marshes.

3

A is incorrect because the word *rest* does not mean "the act of sleeping."

B is incorrect because the word *rest* does not mean "a break from exercise."

C is incorrect because the word *rest* does not mean "a place to stop."

D is correct because the word *rest* means "the part that is left over."

4

A is incorrect because the word *moved* does not mean "changed from one position to another."

B is correct because the word *moved* means "to bring out emotions."

C is incorrect because the word *moved* does not mean "gone from one home to a new home."

D is incorrect because the word *moved* does not mean "to make a formal request."

5

Main Idea: help protect the Everglades

Details: return rare plants and animals; stop the pollution

Read the passage. Then answer the questions.

Taxes Work for You

Our government does things to help us. It opens schools and keeps parks clean. It maintains buildings and roads. It also pays for police and fire departments. People need many of these things. They are important. But they cost money. It costs money to run a school or to pave roads and highways. Where does all this money come from? The answer might surprise you. A lot of it comes from people like your family. The government requires that citizens pay taxes. Some of these taxes pay for things in the community.

It might seem unfair that we have to pay taxes, but without them we would have problems. Children would not have public schools to learn in. There would be no one to care for the outdoor spaces we love. And there would be no fire department to rescue people when there was an emergency. Communities use taxes to pay for services that are needed by many. Tax dollars allow people to have a safe community that everyone can enjoy. Life would be very different if we didn't have taxes!

GO ON →

1 Which sentence **best** describes the author's point of view about taxes?

    A They should be lowered to save people money.

    B They should be raised to help the community.

    C They are needed for communities to be successful.

    D They are not necessary for the services people need.

2 Which sentence from the passage **best** states what the author thinks about the government?

    A "Our government does things to help us."

    B "People need many of these things."

    C "The government requires that citizens pay taxes."

    D "Communities use taxes to pay for services that are needed by many."

GO ON →

Read the passage. Then answer the questions.

Democracy

There are many types of governments in the world. There are some in which the people decide who leads them. There are others in which the people have no say in how the government is run. In the United States, the people have a voice. We are able to vote for our leaders. We have a say in how we are governed. This is called a democracy.

Hundreds of years ago, the American colonies were ruled by England. England's government was a monarchy. That is when a king or queen makes the laws. The people in the American colonies were not free to make their own laws. They were not free to pick their own leaders. The king of England made the people do as he said.

Many people thought this was unfair. They distrusted the king and wanted to separate from England. They wanted to start their own country in America. They also wanted to start a new government. It would allow them to vote for new leaders if they were unhappy. So, the colonists fought for their independence and won! They started their new country as a democracy.

GO ON →

3   Read the sentence from the passage.

Many people thought this was <u>unfair</u>.

What does the word <u>unfair</u> mean?

A   always fair

B   before being fair

C   not fair

D   fair again

4   Read the sentence from the passage.

They <u>distrusted</u> the king and wanted to separate from England.

What does the word <u>distrusted</u> mean?

A   usually trusted

B   the opposite of trusted

C   trusted over and over

D   easily trusted

GO ON →

Read the passage. Then answer the questions.

Saving a Grassland

Otero Mesa is a special place. No other area in the country is quite like it. It stretches as far as the eye can see. Tall grasses sway in the breeze. Desert plants send their flower spikes up toward the sky. It is too dry for trees.

A variety of wildlife calls this grassy land home. Prairie dogs dig their tunnels and dens under the grass. Mule deer and antelope graze on it. Songbirds and eagles fly in the blue skies above it.

Beneath, Otero is special, too. Huge amounts of fresh water lie below the ground.

People have used and lived on this grassland for centuries. Ancient Native American ruins dot the mesa. Some pictures carved on rocks are more than one thousand years old.

Several years ago, the government suggested a plan. It would allow drilling and mining on the grassland. Many people were unhappy with the plan. They were afraid that the plants and animals would be harmed. Hikers, hunters, and ranchers wanted to keep using and enjoying the grassland. Scientists wanted to study its wildlife, rocks, and water. The Apache wanted to protect the ruins of their ancestors.

Many of these people started working together. They wrote letters and e-mails to the government in Washington, D.C. They called their government representatives to ask them to stop the plan. They signed petitions. A petition is a written request signed by many people that asks the government to do something. Americans have the right to petition their government. It is an important right.

This is how our government works. Voters choose people to send to Washington, D.C. These people represent the voters. But they need to know what voters think. They do not want to misunderstand voters' wishes. If they do, they might make laws that voters do not want. People must let the government know what they want.

GO ON →

After many months, a court ruled against the drilling plan. The court told the government to rethink the plan. It said the government must consider the effects on nature before it allowed drilling.

The people who worked against the plan were happy. For now, the people have reclaimed this land as a wilderness area. No one can drill on it. No one can mine on it. But the future of Otero Mesa is still uncertain. Many of these determined people are working together again. They want the government to call the land a wilderness area. That means the animals and plants would be protected. The land could not be used except for recreation. Once again, these people are writing letters and e-mails. They are calling their representatives. They are signing petitions. They want to make sure drilling and mining are never allowed on the Otero Mesa.

GO ON →

5 Which sentence **best** states the author's point of view about Otero Mesa?

   A "No other area in the country is quite like it."

   B "Tall grasses sway in the breeze."

   C "A variety of wildlife calls this grassy land home."

   D "Mule deer and antelope graze on it."

6 Read the sentence from the passage.

   They do not want to <u>misunderstand</u> voters' wishes.

   What does the word <u>misunderstand</u> mean?

   A understand again

   B understand wrongly

   C understand easily

   D understand late

GO ON →

7   Read the paragraph from the passage.

Many of these people started working together. They wrote letters and e-mails to the government in Washington, D.C. They called their government representatives to ask them to stop the plan. They signed petitions. A petition is a written request signed by many people that asks the government to do something. Americans have the right to petition their government. It is an important right.

Which statement explains the author's point of view in the paragraph?

A   Petitions let the government know what people want.

B   Protecting the Otero Mesa is the incorrect thing to do.

C   There are problems with the people's right to petition.

D   The government needs to be changed.

8   Read the sentence from the passage.

The court told the government to <u>rethink</u> the plan.

What does the word <u>rethink</u> mean?

A   think quickly

B   think before

C   think wrongly

D   think again

GO ON →

9   Read the sentence from the passage.

But the future of Otero Mesa is still <u>uncertain</u>.

What does the word <u>uncertain</u> mean?

A   certain before

B   certain again

C   very certain

D   not certain

10   Choose **two** statements below that explain the author's point of view in the passage. Write them in the chart.

Author's Point of View	

Statements:
Otero Mesa is not a protected place.
The government should protect nature.
People should be allowed to drill on natural land.
The government is too busy to listen to our concerns.
Americans should let the government know what they think.

Student Name: _____

Question	Correct Answer	Content Focus	Complexity
1	C	Author's Point of View	DOK 3
2	A	Author's Point of View	DOK 2
3	C	Prefixes: *re-, un-, dis-, mis-*	DOK 1
4	B	Prefixes: *re-, un-, dis-, mis-*	DOK 1
5	A	Author's Point of View	DOK 2
6	B	Prefixes: *re-, un-, dis-, mis-*	DOK 1
7	A	Author's Point of View	DOK 3
8	D	Prefixes: *re-, un-, dis-, mis-*	DOK 1
9	D	Prefixes: *re-, un-, dis-, mis-*	DOK 1
10	see below	Author's Point of View	DOK 3

Comprehension 1, 2, 5, 7, 10	/10	%
Vocabulary 3, 4, 6, 8, 9	/10	%
Total Progress Monitoring Assessment Score	/20	%

10   Students should write the following statements in the chart:
   • The government should protect nature.
   • Americans should let the government know what they think.

Unit 2 Weeks 1–2 Rationales

1

A is incorrect because the author doesn't think taxes should be lowered to save people money.

B is incorrect because the author doesn't think taxes should be raised to help the community.

C is correct because the author thinks taxes are needed for communities to be successful.

D is incorrect because the author thinks taxes are necessary for the services people need.

2

A is correct because the author thinks our government does things to help us.

B is incorrect because the sentence does not best state what the author thinks about the government.

C is incorrect because the sentence does not best state what the author thinks about the government.

D is incorrect because the sentence does not best state what the author thinks about the government.

3

A is incorrect because the word *unfair* does not mean "always fair."

B is incorrect because the word *unfair* does not mean "before being fair."

C is correct because the prefix *un-* means "not."

D is incorrect because the word *unfair* does not mean "fair again."

4

A is incorrect because the word *distrusted* does not mean "usually trusted."

B is correct because the prefix *dis-* means "the opposite of."

C is incorrect because the word *distrusted* does not mean "trusted over and over."

D is incorrect because the word *distrusted* does not mean "easily trusted."

5

A is correct because the author thinks no other area in the country is like Otero Mesa.

B is incorrect because the sentence does not best state what the author thinks about Otero Mesa.

C is incorrect because the sentence does not best state what the author thinks about Otero Mesa.

D is incorrect because the sentence does not best state what the author thinks about Otero Mesa.

6

A is incorrect because the word *misunderstand* does not mean "understand again."

B is correct because the prefix *mis-* means "wrong."

C is incorrect because the word *misunderstand* does not mean "understand easily."

D is incorrect because the word *misunderstand* does not mean "understand late."

7

A is correct because details are provided that show petitions let the government know what people want in the paragraph.

B is incorrect because protecting the Otero Mesa is not shown to be incorrect in the paragraph.

C is incorrect because no problems with the people's right to petition are introduced in the paragraph.

D is incorrect because the author's point of view about the government needing to be changed is not in the paragraph.

8

A is incorrect because the word *rethink* does not mean "think quickly."

B is incorrect because the word *rethink* does not mean "think before."

C is incorrect because the word *rethink* does not mean "think wrongly."

D is correct because the prefix *re-* means "again."

9

A is incorrect because the word *uncertain* does not mean "certain before."

B is incorrect because the word *uncertain* does not mean "certain again."

C is incorrect because the word *uncertain* does not mean "very certain."

D is correct because the prefix *un-* means "not."

10

The following sentences explain the author's point of view:

The government should protect nature

Americans should let the government know what they think.

Read the passage. Then answer the questions.

Going Westward

Brian had lived in Dublin his whole life. He never thought he would ever want to leave. But times were getting tough all across Ireland. There was less and less food. People were going hungry. When he lost his job at the potato farm, he knew he had nothing left to lose.

Brian had heard of others sailing to America. The Americans were building a railroad. It would go from ocean to ocean. Surely, they could use a young man with a strong back. Brian was always willing to do any job, no matter how tough.

So Brian decided to save every penny. He sold everything he had. It was just enough to get a ticket for passage from Ireland to New York City. From there, he headed west to Missouri.

Brian joined other immigrants on the railroad crews. He worked so hard that the bosses kept him on until the last spike was put in. When the railroad was complete, Brian had saved enough money to buy land in Nebraska. He had lost his farming job back in Ireland. Now he had a working farm of his own in America!

GO ON →

1   What is the lesson shown in the passage?

    A Some people are more helpful than others.

    B Success comes when you put in hard work.

    C It's important to not jump to conclusions.

    D Friends will always want you to do well in life.

2   Which sentence from the passage supports the main theme?

    A "When he lost his job at the potato farm, he knew he had nothing left to lose."

    B "The Americans were building a railroad."

    C "It was just enough to get a ticket for passage from Ireland to New York City."

    D "Now he had a working farm of his own in America!"

GO ON →

Read the passage. Then answer the questions.

Mayflower Voyagers

Martin and Lydia Saunders lived in London with their four children. They were unhappy with some of the laws of the land. At that time, all people had to belong to the Church of England. By 1620, Martin and Lydia decided to leave England.

They joined a group of people in search of freedom. Together, they sailed from London to Plymouth, Massachusetts. These people were called Pilgrims. They headed west on a ship called the Mayflower.

It was a rough trip across the ocean. There were strong storms. There were waves as tall as mountains. Most of the family got sick on the journey. The Mayflower sailed for more than two months across the rough seas.

On November 9, 1620, Martin heard someone shout, "Land ho!" Everyone was happy to arrive! But winter was coming. Martin and the others worked as fast as lightning to build homes and other buildings.

At first, it was hard to find food and stay warm. But as the seasons passed, the Saunders family made the new land their home. It was a difficult trip immigrating across the sea, but it was worth it to be free.

GO ON →

3   Read the sentence from the passage.

There were waves as tall as mountains.

What does the sentence help the reader understand about the journey?

A It was slow and tiring.

B It was very dangerous.

C It was repeated over and over.

D It was on a very large ship.

4   Read the sentence from the passage.

Martin and the others worked <u>as fast as lightning</u> to build homes and other buildings.

What does the simile "as fast as lightning" mean?

A without anyone noticing

B in an angry way

C carefully

D as quickly as possible

GO ON →

Read the passage. Then answer the questions.

Grandma Maria's

"Rosa," Grandma Maria said, "take the broom and go sweep the kitchen. I want it to sparkle like a diamond in there."

Rosa frowned and replied, "Grandma, why do we have to clean when we are leaving for America tomorrow?"

Maria looked around at the old restaurant her family had owned for many years. Now the year was 1920, and her son, Sal, had made the decision to leave it all behind. At first, she was angry with him. But then he told her about America and the chance to create a better life for his wife and children. How could she argue with that?

He asked her to go with him. It was at that moment that Maria realized something, like a lightbulb turning on in her head. Her place was with her family. If that was in America, then she would start a new life there with them.

"Grandma?" asked Rosa again. She was still waiting for an answer.

"Because I will not leave my restaurant a mess, my sweet!" she said with a slap of her napkin. "Now get that broom."

Rosa giggled and skipped off to the kitchen, just as Sal charged into the restaurant like a bull.

"Mama!" he shouted, waving a piece of paper excitedly.

"What is it, Sal?" asked Maria. "My goodness, is everything all right?"

"Yes, Mama, it's wonderful!" he said as he handed her the paper.

"What is this?" she asked, still confused. Then she saw the word LEASE in big letters at the top of the paper. It looked like a lease to a building in New York, the place where they were moving. Looking up, she saw pride in her son's eyes.

GO ON →

"It's our new restaurant, Mama, a chance to start a new tradition in America. We can rebuild the family place there and serve the same meals and live the same life that you love!"

Sal noticed that Grandma Maria had sat down and was crying.

"What is it, Mama? Don't you want a restaurant in America?"

She nodded and laughed before taking her son's hand.

"My son, how proud I am of you. I have been upset these past weeks because we are leaving our history behind. Meanwhile, you have found a way to bring it with us. Yes, of course I want a restaurant in America. And yes, of course I am happy! But it is not because we will have the same life. It is because we will have a new one with the chance to share many more happy memories."

Grandma Maria hugged her son and dried her tears. Then she asked, "So what do you want to call our new restaurant in America?"

Sal smiled as he said, "That part is easy, Mama. We will call it 'Grandma Maria's.'"

GO ON →

5 Read the sentence from the passage.

"I want it to sparkle like a diamond in there."

What does the simile "sparkle like a diamond" help the reader understand about Grandma Maria?

A She has never worked in the restaurant.

B She keeps jewels in the restaurant.

C She wants the restaurant very clean.

D She has already cleaned the restaurant.

6 What lesson does the passage show?

A People change as they get older.

B You should try to learn from your mistakes.

C Family is the most important thing.

D Friends are there for you when you need them.

7 Read the sentence from the passage.

It was at that moment that Maria realized something, like a lightbulb turning on in her head.

What does the simile "like a lightbulb turning on" mean?

A in a sudden way

B in a painful way

C easy to forget

D hard to see

GO ON →

8 How do Grandma Maria's actions support the theme in the passage?

    A She is upset about leaving behind her restaurant.

    B She is willing to go with her family to America.

    C She wants Rosa to clean up the restaurant.

    D She is angry with Sal for wanting to leave.

9 Read the paragraph from the passage.

Rosa giggled and skipped off to the kitchen, just as Sal charged into the restaurant <u>like a bull</u>.

What does the simile "like a bull" show about Sal?

    A He has been playing with his children.

    B He is large and tends to knock things over.

    C He is angry about something.

    D He has something important to say.

10 Read the paragraph below. Underline the sentence that **best** states the main theme of the passage.

"My son, how proud I am of you. I have been upset these past weeks because we are leaving our history behind. Meanwhile, you have found a way to bring it with us. Yes, of course I want a restaurant in America. And yes, of course I am happy! But it is not because we will have the same life. It is because we will have a new one with the chance to share many more happy memories."

STOP

Answer Key

Student Name: _____

Question	Correct Answer	Content Focus	Complexity
1	B	Theme	DOK 3
2	D	Theme	DOK 3
3	B	Figurative Language: Similes	DOK 2
4	D	Figurative Language: Similes	DOK 2
5	C	Figurative Language: Similes	DOK 2
6	C	Theme	DOK 3
7	A	Figurative Language: Similes	DOK 2
8	B	Theme	DOK 3
9	D	Figurative Language: Similes	DOK 2
10	see below	Theme	DOK 3

Comprehension 1, 2, 6, 8, 10	/10	%
Vocabulary 3, 4, 5, 7, 9	/10	%
Total Progress Monitoring Assessment Score	/20	%

10 Students should underline the following sentence in the paragraph:
- "It is because we will have a new one with the chance to share many more happy memories."

Copyright © McGraw-Hill Education

Unit 2 Weeks 3–4 Rationales

1

A is incorrect because the lesson isn't that some people are more helpful than others.

B is correct because the lesson is that success comes when you put in hard work.

C is incorrect because the lesson isn't to not jump to conclusions.

D is incorrect because the lesson isn't that friends will always want you to do well in life.

2

A is incorrect because this sentence does not support the theme of hard work leads to success.

B is incorrect because this sentence does not support the theme of hard work leads to success.

C is incorrect because this sentence does not support the theme of hard work leads to success.

D is correct because this sentence supports the theme of hard work leads to success.

3

A is incorrect because this sentence does not help the reader understand that the journey was slow and tiring.

B is correct because this sentence helps the reader understand that the journey was very dangerous.

C is incorrect because this sentence does not help the reader understand that the journey was repeated over and over.

D is incorrect because this sentence does not help the reader understand that the journey was on a very large ship.

4

A is incorrect because "as fast as lightning" does not mean "without anyone noticing."

B is incorrect because "as fast as lightning" does not mean "in an angry way."

C is incorrect because "as fast as lightning" does not mean "carefully."

D is correct because the simile "as fast as lightning" means "as quickly as possible."

5

A is incorrect because the simile "sparkle like a diamond" does not mean "never worked before."

B is incorrect because the simile "sparkle like a diamond" does not mean "keeping jewels."

C is correct because the simile "sparkle like a diamond" means "very clean."

D is incorrect because the simile "sparkle like a diamond" does not mean "already cleaned."

6

A is incorrect because there is no evidence to show that people change as they get older.

B is incorrect because there is no evidence to show that people should learn from their mistakes.

C is correct because the passage shows that family is the most important thing.

D is incorrect because there is no evidence to support that friends are there when you need them.

7

A is correct because the simile "like a lightbulb turning on" means "in a sudden way."

B is incorrect because "like a lightbulb turning on" does not mean "in a painful way."

C is incorrect because "like a lightbulb turning on" does not mean "easy to forget."

D is incorrect because "like a lightbulb turning on" does not mean "hard to see."

8

A is incorrect because this doesn't support the theme of family being important.

B is correct because this supports the theme of family being important.

C is incorrect because this doesn't support the theme of family being important.

D is incorrect because this doesn't support the theme of family being important.

9

A is incorrect because "like a bull" doesn't mean Sal has been playing.

B is incorrect because "like a bull" doesn't mean Sal is large and knocks things over.

C is incorrect because "like a bull" doesn't mean Sal is angry about something.

D is correct because Sal comes in "like a bull" because he has something important to say.

10

The sentence that states the main theme of the passage is at the end of the paragraph:

"It is because we will have a new one with the chance to share many more happy memories."

Read the poem. Then answer the questions.

Number Dance

I know that I can add well—
That two plus four is six.
But when I try to multiply,
My mind starts playing tricks.

5 The numbers all escape me
Like fireflies at night
And even if I try my best,
I still can't do it right!

I multiply by one just fine,
10 But then I try by two.
My brain is like a scrambled egg—
It's just so hard to do!

Now, two times two is four, I think.
But what is two times three?
15 The answer slips away just like
A squirrel runs up a tree.

The numbers all start whirling
Like dancers on a stage.
They jump and spin and won't stay put.
20 They leap right off the page!

"Practice, Mark," my teacher says.
"It's really just the same
As if you were a pitcher
Preparing for a game."

25 I get my team together—
Miguel, Nick, Jane, and me.
We start with two times two and then
Go on to two times three.

GO ON →

We've got the threes and fours done.
30   We've learned six, seven, eight—
Team Number's going down now,
Team Kid is doing great!

We practice hard together
And memorize them all,
35   Until at last I multiply
As well as I play ball.

GO ON →

1   Which line shows who the speaker of the poem is?

    A   I know that I can add well—

    B   My mind starts playing tricks.

    C   "Practice, Mark," my teacher says.

    D   Miguel, Nick, Jane, and me.

2   Read the line from the poem.

My brain is <u>like a scrambled egg</u>—

Based on the simile "like a scrambled egg," how does the speaker feel?

    A   confused

    B   hungry

    C   excited

    D   angry

3   Read the lines from the poem.

"It's really just the same
As if you were a pitcher
Preparing for a game."

Why does the teacher compare multiplying to preparing for a baseball game?

    A   to show that multiplication is used a lot in baseball

    B   to show that multiplying is harder than playing baseball

    C   to show that both multiplying and pitching take practice

    D   to show that all baseball pitchers are good at multiplying

GO ON →

4 Which sentence **best** describes what the speaker thinks about math at the end of the poem?

    A The speaker thinks it's difficult.

    B The speaker thinks it's confusing.

    C The speaker thinks it's helpful.

    D The speaker thinks it's easy.

5 Complete the chart. Write **two** statements with which the speaker would **most likely** agree. Choose the statements from the box below.

Point of View

Statements:
Teachers can help students understand math.
Multiplying confuses everyone.
Practicing can help you multiply well.
Multiplying is more fun than baseball.
Baseball players always have to multiply.

Answer Key

Student Name: _____

Question	Correct Answer	Content Focus	Complexity
1	C	Point of View	DOK 2
2	A	Figurative Language: Similes	DOK 2
3	C	Figurative Language: Similes	DOK 2
4	D	Point of View	DOK 2
5	see below	Point of View	DOK 3

Comprehension 1, 4, 5	/6	%
Vocabulary 2, 3	/4	%
Total Progress Monitoring Assessment Score	/10	%

5 Students should write the following statements in the chart:
   • Teachers can help students understand math.
   • Practicing can help you multiply well.

Unit 2 Week 5 Rationales

1

A is incorrect because the reader doesn't know who the speaker is from this line.

B is incorrect because the reader doesn't know who the speaker is from this line.

C is correct because this line tells us the speaker is Mark.

D is incorrect because the reader doesn't know who the speaker is from this line.

2

A is correct because the simile "like a scrambled egg" means "confused."

B is incorrect because "like a scrambled egg" does not mean "hungry."

C is incorrect because "like a scrambled egg" does not mean "excited."

D is incorrect because "like a scrambled egg" does not mean "angry."

3

A is incorrect because the comparison is not made to show that multiplication is used a lot in baseball.

B is incorrect because the comparison is not made to show that multiplying is harder than playing baseball.

C is correct because the comparison shows that both multiplying and pitching take practice.

D is incorrect because the comparison is not made to show that all pitchers are good at multiplying.

4

A is incorrect because the speaker doesn't think math is difficult.

B is incorrect because the speaker doesn't think math is confusing.

C is incorrect because the speaker doesn't think math is helpful.

D is correct because the speaker thinks math is easy at the end of the poem.

5

The statements that show the speaker's point of view are the following:

Teachers can help students understand math.

Practicing can help you multiply well.

Read the passage. Then answer the questions.

Important Pictures in the Sky

When stars group together, they form super groups called constellations. People have been amazed by constellations for a long time. It's fun to look at star groups because they have special patterns and names. People have named them for their shapes, such as Pisces for fishes or Leo for a lion. You may have heard of some, such as Orion or Pegasus. Their patterns help you see star groups in the night sky. They are interesting to look at, but constellations are important for another reason.

One way that they are important is that they serve as maps. People have used constellations as maps for thousands of years. Sailors used the stars to guide them while at sea. They knew the stars always followed the same path in the sky. This helped sailors know which direction they needed to go to get to their destinations.

We also use constellations to locate stars that don't change position very much. Their position stays the same night after night. For example, we know the North Star always points north. For that reason, it is used by many people to find their way home!

GO ON →

1   What is the main idea of the passage?

   A   Constellations are groups of stars in the night sky.

   B   Constellations are in the same place on any night.

   C   Constellations are interesting and useful to people.

   D   Constellations are named for their shapes.

2   What does the second paragraph help readers understand?

   A   People used the constellations like maps.

   B   People gave one constellation the name Orion.

   C   People created stories about constellations.

   D   People used the North Star when they were lost.

GO ON →

Read the passage. Then answer the questions.

A Blanket for Planet Earth

People grab a coat or an umbrella before going outdoors. Their lives are guided by the weather. This has to do with Earth's atmosphere. Earth is surrounded by gases that help to protect it and the things that live on it. The gases act like a blanket around the planet.

The layer of atmosphere that we live in is called the troposphere. Life can exist in this layer. People walk around, plants grow, and birds fly freely. That is because this layer of gases has air in it. Without air, there would be no life on Earth. Air has the oxygen that we breathe.

Nearly all weather occurs in this lowest layer of the atmosphere. The troposphere goes through many weather changes. One day, you might wear a coat because there is a chilly breeze, but another day you might feel warm because the air is hot and heavy.

Even though the weather changes, we are safe under the troposphere. It seals the planet and keeps us from being burned by the sun. It also shields us from the coldness of space. It provides protection for everyone!

GO ON →

3   Read the sentence from the passage.

People walk around, plants grow, and birds fly <u>freely</u>.

The suffix *-ly* means "in a certain way." What does <u>freely</u> tell about how the birds fly?

A   They are able to fly.

B   They do not fly at all.

C   They fly only at night.

D   They do not fly well.

4   Read the sentence from the passage.

One day, you might wear a coat because there is a <u>chilly</u> breeze, but another day you might feel warm because the air is heavy and hot.

What does the word <u>chilly</u> mean?

A   weak

B   cool

C   warm

D   strong

GO ON →

Read the passage. Then answer the questions.

Our Closest Star

A tiny white light twinkles in the night sky, and a large yellow ball blazes brightly during the day. Which of those objects is a star? You answered correctly if you said, "Both!" The daytime light is the sun, of course. It looks very different from the little lights you see at night, so it is hard to believe that the sun is the same kind of object.

A star is a ball of extremely hot gases. The gases are so hot that they burn and glow. A very hot day here on Earth is about 100 degrees, but gases at the sun's surface are about one hundred times hotter than that. Like all stars, the sun is even hotter inside. At the sun's center, it is about 27 million degrees!

Stars do not all have the same temperature though, and they also differ in color and brightness. The hottest stars glow bluish white, and the coolest stars glow coppery red. The sun is actually a star of ordinary temperature and brightness. Ordinary stars glow yellow.

Stars are not all the same size either. Some stars are so large that they are called super-giants, while other stars are much smaller. The sun is a star of ordinary size.

Then why does the sun look so much larger than any other star, and why does it feel so warm? That is because it is much closer to Earth than any other star. The closer an object is to you, the larger it looks. The sun is about 93 million miles away. That is very far, but it is close if you are talking about distances in the universe. Other stars are much, much farther away. The time it takes for light to travel through space and reach Earth is quite lengthy.

All in all, our sun is a very ordinary star, but to us on Earth, it does not appear that way. To us, the sun is huge and bright.

GO ON →

Just how big is the sun compared to Earth? Picture this: If the sun were the size of a basketball, Earth would be the size of the head of a pin! More than a million planets the size of Earth could fit in the sun, and there might even be space left over for a moon or two.

The sun's brightness is also powerful to us. It is so bright that you should not look directly at it. If you did, it could damage your eyes. The sun blocks light from the other stars, which is why you cannot see other stars during the day.

Although the sun is an ordinary star in the universe, it is anything but ordinary to those who live here on Earth!

GO ON →

5 Complete the chart by writing the main idea of the passage and the details that support the main idea. Use all of the sentences from the box below.

Main Idea:
Detail:
Detail:
Detail:

Sentences:

The sun is closer to Earth than any other star.

The sun is a star that is important to life on Earth.

Stars have different temperatures and colors.

Stars are made of gases that give off heat.

GO ON →

6   Read the sentence from the passage.

A tiny white light twinkles in the night sky, and a large yellow ball blazes <u>brightly</u> during the day.

What does the word <u>brightly</u> mean?

A   to make bright

B   in a bright way

C   without brightness

D   being the brightest

7   What is the sun made of?

A   bits of dirt

B   hot liquids

C   burning gases

D   many little stars

8   Read the sentence from the passage.

The time it takes for light to travel through space and reach Earth is quite <u>lengthy</u>.

The suffix *-y* means "full of." What does the word <u>lengthy</u> mean?

A   too long

B   not long enough

C   becoming long

D   very long

GO ON →

9   Read the sentence from the passage.

It is so bright that you should not look <u>directly</u> at it.

What does it mean to look at the sun <u>directly</u>?

   A   stare right at the sun

   B   glance quickly at the sun

   C   remember seeing the sun

   D   look at the sun more than once

10   **Which sentence best states the main idea of the passage?**

   A   "It looks very different from the little lights you see at night, so it is hard to believe that the sun is the same kind of object."

   B   "Like all stars, the sun is even hotter inside."

   C   "The closer an object is to you, the larger it looks."

   D   "Although the sun is an ordinary star in the universe, it is anything but ordinary to those who live here on Earth!"

Answer Key

Student Name: _____

Question	Correct Answer	Content Focus	Complexity
1	C	Main Idea and Key Details	DOK 2
2	A	Main Idea and Key Details	DOK 2
3	A	Suffixes: -y, -ly	DOK 1
4	B	Suffixes: -y, -ly	DOK 1
5	see below	Main Idea and Key Details	DOK 2
6	B	Suffixes: -y, -ly	DOK 1
7	C	Main Idea and Key Details	DOK 2
8	D	Suffixes: -y, -ly	DOK 1
9	A	Suffixes: -y, -ly	DOK 1
10	D	Main Idea and Key Details	DOK 2

Comprehension 1, 2, 5, 7, 10	/10	%
Vocabulary 3, 4, 6, 8, 9	/10	%
Total Progress Monitoring Assessment Score	/20	%

5 Students should complete the chart as follows:
- Main Idea: The sun is a star that is important to life on Earth.
- Detail: Stars have different temperatures and colors.
- Detail: Stars are made of gases that give off heat.
- Detail: The sun is closer to Earth than any other star.

Unit 3 Weeks 1–2 Rationales

1

A is incorrect because the detail supports a key idea that constellations are groups of stars.

B is incorrect because the detail supports a key idea that constellations seem to hold their position in the sky.

C is correct because the first paragraph explains why constellations are interesting, and the second and third paragraphs tell how constellations help people.

D is incorrect because the detail supports a key idea that people name constellations based on their shape.

2

A is correct because the paragraph discusses how people use the stars as maps to guide them.

B is incorrect because the detail is not explained but is related to information in the first paragraph.

C is incorrect because the detail is related to constellations but is not explained in the paragraph.

D is incorrect because this information is provided in the third paragraph of the passage.

3

A is correct because the word *freely* includes the root *free* and the suffix *-ly*, which suggests that birds are free to fly whenever they wish.

B is incorrect because the suffix *-ly* turns the adjective *free* into an adverb. If a bird flies *freely*, it is free to fly.

C is incorrect because the adverb *freely* contains the root *free*, indicating that the birds are free to fly when they wish.

D is incorrect because the word *freely* and its root word *free* do not suggest that birds do not fly well.

4

A is incorrect because the suffix *-y* means "having," so a *chilly* breeze has a chill in it; it is not necessarily weak.

B is correct because the word *chilly* means "having a chill," so a chilly breeze is cool.

C is incorrect because the suffix *-y* means "having," so a chilly breeze would not be warm.

D is incorrect because the root *chill* and suffix *-y* tell that *chilly* has to do with the temperature of the breeze, not its strength.

5

The main idea of the passage is that the sun is a star that is important to life on Earth. All of the other sentences in the box support this main idea.

6

A is incorrect because the suffix *-ly* means "in a certain way," so "blazes brightly" means the sun blazes "in a bright way" instead of "to make bright" (*-en*).

B is correct because the suffix *-ly* means "in a certain way," so "blazes brightly" means the sun blazes "in a bright way."

C is incorrect because the suffix *-ly* means "in a certain way," so "blazes brightly" means the sun blazes "in a bright way" instead of "without brightness" (*-less*).

D is incorrect because the suffix *-ly* means "in a certain way," so "blazes brightly" means the sun blazes "in a bright way" instead of "being the most bright" (*-est*).

7

A is incorrect because a star is made up of "extremely hot gases."

B is incorrect because the sun is a star, and stars are made up of gases.

C is correct because the second paragraph explains that a star is made up of hot gases and that a star's gases "are so hot that they burn and glow."

D is incorrect because nothing suggests that the sun is made up of smaller stars.

8

A is incorrect because the suffix *-y* means "having or being," so a "lengthy time" is a very long time but not "too long."

B is incorrect because the suffix *-y* means "having or being," so a "lengthy time" is a very long time instead of "not long enough."

C is incorrect because the suffix *-y* means "having or being," so a "lengthy time" is a very long time instead of "becoming long" (*-en*).

D is correct because the word *lengthy* means "being long," so a "lengthy time" is a very long time.

9

A is correct because the suffix *-ly* means "in a certain way," so "not look directly" cautions not to look right at the sun or not to look at the sun in a direct way.

B is incorrect because the suffix *-ly* means "in a certain way," so "not look directly" cautions not to look at the sun in a direct way rather than to look at it quickly.

C is incorrect because the suffix *-ly* means "in a certain way," so "not look directly" cautions not to look at the sun in a direct way rather than to look at it reflectively.

D is incorrect because the suffix *-ly* means "in a certain way," so "not look directly" cautions not to look at the sun in a direct way rather than to look at it repeatedly.

10

A is incorrect because this is a detail that describes how the sun is a star although it looks very different.

B is incorrect because this is a detail that supports the key idea that the sun is a star.

C is incorrect because this is a detail that explains how perspective makes an object seem larger when it is closer.

D is correct because the main idea of the passage is that the sun, while ordinary among stars, is extraordinary to people on Earth as a source of heat and light.

Read the passage. Then answer the questions.

Stories from a Hidden World

Juan longed to be a great storyteller, but he had no stories to tell.

Little did Juan know that a jaguar cub was hiding high in a forest tree. *I miss my family*, sighed the cub, who had become separated from its mother.

Finally, the cub decided to come down and try a path. Juan happened to be on the same path to fetch water from the river.

The two met. Juan was afraid of the cat, but the jaguar was curious about Juan.

"Please don't hurt me," begged Juan. "I see you are a fierce hunter!"

"That's right!" roared the jaguar, pretending to be brave. "All the animals fear me —wild pigs, monkeys, sloths, and more!"

"You know all of those creatures?" asked Juan.

"Of course!" boasted the young cat. "I could tell you many amazing stories, such as the fight with the mighty river caiman!"

"Oh, I would love to hear that story!" said Juan.

"Then stay with me until my family arrives, and in turn, I will tell you stories," promised the cub.

Juan retold the jaguar's tales in his village, and he became a great storyteller because of his unlikely friend.

GO ON →

1   Read the paragraph from the passage.

Little did Juan know that a jaguar cub was hiding high in a forest tree. *I miss my family,* sighed the cub, who had become separated from its mother.

What problem does the jaguar cub have in the paragraph?

A   The cub is stuck in a forest tree.

B   The cub is hiding from predators.

C   The cub is lost from its mother.

D   The cub is afraid of the other animals.

2   How does the jaguar solve Juan's problem?

A   by helping Juan find his way back home

B   by keeping Juan safe until his mother returns

C   by listening to Juan's story about the river caiman

D   by telling Juan many stories about the forest

GO ON →

Read the passage. Then answer the questions.

Anansi Steals All the Wisdom in the World

An African Folktale

Anansi was a clever spider but he was not very wise, so he came up with a plan to become so. He decided to steal his wisdom. Anansi picked up a hollow gourd and said to himself, "If I fill this empty gourd with important wisdom, then it will make me wiser than everyone else!"

So Anansi went through the forest to gather wisdom from each animal. As they spoke, he held up his gourd to get the wise words. Once the gourd was full, Anansi decided to carry it up a big tree. He did not want anyone to steal it from him! But it was too difficult for Anansi to carry the gourd.

All at once, Anansi's son came upon him and asked, "Father, why don't you just tie the gourd to your back?"

Anansi smiled at his son's wise words, and he realized that wisdom was best used if shared with others. So he climbed the tree all the way to the very top. Then he held the gourd up to the sky as the wind carried the wisdom away. And that is how wisdom came to the land.

GO ON →

3   Read the sentence from the passage.

Anansi picked up a <u>hollow</u> gourd and said to himself, "If I fill this empty gourd with important wisdom, then it will make me wiser than everyone else!"

Which word from the sentence is a synonym for the word <u>hollow</u>?

A   empty

B   important

C   wiser

D   else

4   Read the sentences from the passage.

So Anansi went through the forest to <u>gather</u> wisdom from each animal. As they spoke, he held up his gourd to get the wise words.

Which word from the sentences helps the reader know what <u>gather</u> means?

A   went

B   through

C   spoke

D   get

GO ON →

Read the passage. Then answer the questions.

The Lion and the Mouse
A Retelling of Aesop's Fable

One day, a tiny gray mouse scurried along when she came upon a great lion dozing in the forest. In a hurry to get home, she didn't take the time to go around the lion. Instead, she ran up the lion's tail, over his back, through his mane, and down his nose. By that time, the lion had awakened and opened one eye. When the mouse leapt off the lion's nose onto the ground, the lion took a mighty swipe with his paw. It landed on the mouse's tail, stopping her in her tracks.

"How dare you crawl on the King of the Beasts!" the lion roared.

The mouse was terrified that the lion would crush her. She squeaked, "Oh please, great lion, I was in a hurry to get home and did not mean any harm. I did not intend to wake you."

"But wake me you did," the lion replied, "and now with my powerful paw I will—"

"Wait!" pleaded the mouse. "If you set me free, one day I will repay you. I will help you, I promise."

"Hah!" the lion laughed. "How can a mouse as tiny as you ever help a great beast like me?"

But the lion was so amused by the idea that he decided to let the mouse go. She scampered away into the forest.

Many days later, three men entered the forest seeking to bring back a lion. Creeping along, they observed the mighty lion napping once again. When they saw him, they quickly threw a large rope net over him and tied the net to a tree. The lion twisted and turned and pulled with all his strength, but he could not break the ropes. He roared his loudest roar, but the hunters were not frightened. They smiled and left to get a cart to carry the lion off.

GO ON →

Progress Monitoring Assessments

Far away, the little mouse heard the lion's roar and came running. "Oh, no!" she cried when she saw the lion trapped in the rope net. "You've been captured!" Then, she immediately began to chew through the net. She used her sharp teeth to cut away first one rope and then another, and soon the lion was freed from the snare.

The lion lifted the mouse gently up on his paw. "If it were not for you, I would no longer be the King of the Beasts," he said softly. "You were right, little one. Even a creature as tiny as you can help a mighty animal like me."

GO ON →

5 Read the sentences from the passage.

One day, a tiny gray mouse <u>scurried</u> along when she came upon a great lion dozing in the forest. In a hurry to get home, she didn't take the time to go around the lion. Instead, she ran up the lion's tail, over his back, through his mane, and down his nose.

Which word from the sentences is a synonym for the word <u>scurried</u>?

A ran

B back

C through

D down

6 Which sentence **best** states the mouse's problem in the passage?

A "Instead, she ran up the lion's tail, over his back, through his mane, and down his nose."

B "When the mouse leapt off the lion's nose onto the ground, the lion took a mighty swipe with his paw."

C "Many days later, three men entered the forest seeking to bring back a lion."

D "She used her sharp teeth to cut away first one rope and then another, and soon the lion was freed from the snare."

GO ON →

7   How does the mouse's problem with the lion get solved?

   A   The lion decides to take a nap.

   B   The lion gets captured by hunters.

   C   The lion learns to chew through rope.

   D   The lion is amused and frees the mouse.

8   Read the sentences from the passage.

Many days later, three men entered the forest seeking to bring back a lion. Creeping along, they <u>observed</u> the mighty lion napping once again. When they saw him, they quickly threw a large rope net over him and tied the net to a tree.

Which word from the sentences is a synonym for <u>observed</u>?

   A   entered

   B   saw

   C   threw

   D   tied

GO ON →

9   Complete the chart to show if **each** event is a problem or a solution. Draw an X in the correct box for **each** event.

	Problem	Solution
The mouse wakes the sleeping lion.		
The hunters catch the lion in a net.		
The lion cannot twist free of the ropes.		
The mouse chews through the net.		

10   Read the sentences from the passage.

Far away, the little mouse heard the lion's roar and came running. "Oh, no!" she cried when she saw the lion trapped in the rope net. "You've been captured!"

Which word from the sentences gives a clue to the meaning of captured?

A   little

B   heard

C   came

D   trapped

Answer Key

Student Name: _____

Question	Correct Answer	Content Focus	Complexity
1	C	Problem and Solution	DOK 2
2	D	Problem and Solution	DOK 2
3	A	Context Clues: Synonyms	DOK 2
4	D	Context Clues: Synonyms	DOK 2
5	A	Context Clues: Synonyms	DOK 2
6	B	Problem and Solution	DOK 2
7	D	Problem and Solution	DOK 2
8	B	Context Clues: Synonyms	DOK 2
9	see below	Problem and Solution	DOK 2
10	D	Context Clues: Synonyms	DOK 2

Comprehension 1, 2, 6, 7, 9	/10	%
Vocabulary 3, 4, 5, 8, 10	/10	%
Total Progress Monitoring Assessment Score	/20	%

9 Students should put an X in the following boxes for each event:
- The mouse wakes the sleeping lion. – Problem
- The hunters catch the lion in a net. – Problem
- The lion cannot twist free of the ropes. – Problem
- The mouse chews through the net. – Solution

Unit 3 Weeks 3-4 Rationales

1

A is incorrect because the cub is not stuck and can climb down.

B is incorrect because the problem is not that the cub is hiding from predators.

C is correct because the paragraph explains that the jaguar misses its mother.

D is incorrect because the cub scares other animals, not the other way around.

2

A is incorrect because the jaguar tells Juan stories; it does not help Juan get home.

B is incorrect because the jaguar is the one who wants company while it waits for its mother.

C is incorrect because the jaguar is the one who says that he has an amazing story about the fight with the mighty river caiman.

D is correct because Juan's problem is that he wants to be a great storyteller, but he does not know any stories; the jaguar gives him stories to tell others.

3

A is correct because the word *empty* is used to describe the gourd again right after it is identified as a *hollow* gourd.

B is incorrect because the word *important* is used to describe the wisdom, not the gourd.

C is incorrect because the word *wiser* is used to describe Anansi, not the gourd.

D is incorrect because the word *else* is not used to describe the gourd.

4

A is incorrect because the word *went* is used to explain how Anansi moved in the forest.

B is incorrect because the word *through* is used to explain how Anansi moved in the forest.

C is incorrect because the word *spoke* is used in relation to Anansi talking to the animals.

D is correct because the words *get* the *wise words* mean the same thing as *gather wisdom* in the previous sentence.

5

A is correct because both *scurried* and *ran* are used to show how the mouse moves quickly.

B is incorrect because the word *back* does not describe how the mouse moves.

C is incorrect because the word *through* does not describe how the mouse moves, but rather where.

D is incorrect because the word *down* does not describe how the mouse moves, but rather where.

6

A is incorrect because the sentence shows what the mouse does before her problem begins.

B is correct because the mouse's problem is getting caught by the lion's paw.

C is incorrect because this sentence relates to the lion's problem at the end of the passage.

D is incorrect because the sentence shows how the mouse solves the lion's problem.

7

A is incorrect because the lion taking a nap is not a solution for the mouse.

B is incorrect because the lion getting captured is a problem for the lion and not a solution for the mouse.

C is incorrect because the mouse chews through the rope to save the lion and solve his problem.

D is correct because the mouse's promise of help is the amusing solution to her problem of angering the lion.

8

A is incorrect because the word *entered* describes what the men do before they begin to observe the lion.

B is correct because both *observed* and *saw* are used to show that the men notice the lion.

C is incorrect because the word *threw* is used to describe what the men do with the net.

D is incorrect because the word *tied* helps to explain how the men capture the lion.

9

The first statement is a problem for the mouse because she has angered the lion.

The second statement is a problem for the lion because he has been caught.

The third statement is a problem for the lion because he cannot free himself.

The fourth statement is a solution for the lion because the mouse is able to free him.

10

A is incorrect because the word *little* is a description of the mouse.

B is incorrect because the word *heard* shows how the mouse knows the lion is in distress.

C is incorrect because the word *came* shows the action of the mouse, not what is happening to the lion.

D is correct because the mouse says "You've been *captured*!" right after the passage explains that the lion is *trapped*. The mouse's words reiterate what was just previously described.

Read the passage. Then answer the questions.

Pasta Comes to America

Many Americans find it enjoyable to make and eat pasta dishes. Pasta can be long and thin or short and thick. It can even come in shapes like wheels or stars. The names of different types of pasta often describe the way the noodle looks. For example, the word *spaghetti* means "little strings" in Italian. Some people eat pasta with cheese sauce or tomato sauce, and others love it with meat sauce or even just a little oil.

People who like pasta are thankful to Italian Americans. They helped bring pasta to America. Italians first came to America more than one hundred years ago. Many Italians came to live in the big cities in America and often they would live together in their own neighborhoods. That is why many big cities today have a neighborhood called "Little Italy."

Italians loved many things about America, but they did not always like the food in their new country. They missed the food from Italy, especially pasta. They wanted to add fresh vegetables and spices to their sauces. They liked the hard cheeses that they could cook with pasta. They also liked fruit and would eat it with pasta.

This was a different way of eating than most Americans were used to. They did not often use fresh fruits and vegetables in their cooking. And pasta was new to them, too.

Italian Americans found ways to get the foods they liked. First, they planted vegetables and spices in their own gardens. Then, they bought cheeses and pasta that came from faraway Italy.

Then war broke out. Pasta and cheese could not be shipped all the way from Italy. Pasta factories began to open in America. They could make the pasta that Italians wanted.

GO ON →

Progress Monitoring Assessments

As a result, there was a lot of pasta being made in America. It did not cost much money to buy. Then it was discovered that pasta was healthy. Recipes for homemade pasta meals were included in cookbooks and magazines, and Americans began to eat pasta at mealtimes in their homes. Spaghetti and meatballs became a favorite meal!

Italian Americans started to open pasta restaurants and called them spaghetti houses. Italian restaurants soon became very popular. People liked these restaurants. It made them feel like they were in Italy. Even today, Americans enjoy eating at Italian restaurants.

GO ON →

1 Write **each** event in the chart to show the correct order of events.

Order of Events

1	
2	
3	
4	

Events

People bought Italian cheeses and pasta.	People planted vegetable gardens.
People opened Italian restaurants in America.	Factory workers began making pasta in America.

2 Read the sentence from the passage.

Many Americans find it <u>enjoyable</u> to make and eat pasta dishes.

Using the suffix *-able*, what does the word <u>enjoyable</u> mean?

A the process of enjoying

B the result of enjoying

C a person who enjoys

D can be enjoyed

GO ON →

3   Read the following list.

> 1.   Italians arrived in America.
>
> 2.
>
> 3.   Italians found ways to get foods they liked.
>
> 4.   Americans began eating pasta.

Which detail from the passage belongs in the blank?

A   Italians missed eating pasta.

B   Italians opened spaghetti houses.

C   Americans went to Italian restaurants.

D   People could not ship cheese from far away.

4   Read the sentence from the passage.

People who like pasta are <u>thankful</u> to Italian Americans.

What does the word <u>thankful</u> mean?

A   full of thanks

B   without thanks

C   trying to show thanks

D   having some thanks

5   What happened after people found out that pasta was healthy?

A   Hard cheeses were brought over from Italy.

B   Recipes for pasta meals were found in cookbooks.

C   Pasta factories opened to make it easier to buy pasta.

D   Italians planted spices in their gardens.

Answer Key

Student Name: _____

Question	Correct Answer	Content Focus	Complexity
1	see below	Sequence	DOK 1
2	D	Suffixes: *-able, -ful, -less*	DOK 1
3	A	Sequence	DOK 2
4	A	Suffixes: *-able, -ful, -less*	DOK 1
5	B	Sequence	DOK 2

Comprehension 1, 3, 5	/6	%
Vocabulary 2, 4	/4	%
Total Progress Monitoring Assessment Score	/10	%

1   Students should write the events in the following order:
- 1 – People planted vegetable gardens.
- 2 – People bought Italian cheeses and pasta.
- 3 – Factory workers began making pasta in America.
- 4 – People opened Italian restaurants in America.

Unit 3 Week 5 Rationales

1

The following order reflects the order of events described in the passage:

Event 1: People planted vegetable gardens.

Event 2: People bought Italian cheeses and pasta.

Event 3: Factory workers began making pasta in America.

Event 4: People opened Italian restaurants in America.

2

A is incorrect because the suffix *-ment* has the meaning of "process of."

B is incorrect because the suffix *-tion* has the meaning of "result of."

C is incorrect because the suffix *-or* has the meaning of "person who."

D is correct because the suffix *-able* has the meaning of "can be done," or "can be enjoyed."

3

A is correct because the passage states, "They missed the food from Italy, especially pasta."

B is incorrect because there were no spaghetti houses when immigrants arrived in America; those came much after the war.

C is incorrect because people going to Italian restaurants is mentioned as happening after the fourth point on the list.

D is incorrect because people not being able to import cheeses happens after the third point on the list when war breaks out.

4

A is correct because the suffix *-ful* means "full of" so "thankful" means "full of thanks."

B is incorrect because adding suffix *-less* gives the meaning of "without."

C is incorrect because adding suffix *-ive* gives the meaning of "tending toward action."

D is incorrect because adding suffix *-ful* gives the meaning of "full of" instead of "having some."

5

A is incorrect because hard cheeses were brought over before the war and before pasta was found to be healthy.

B is correct because the passage states, "Recipes for homemade pasta meals were included in cookbooks and magazines..." after it was found that pasta is healthy.

C is incorrect because pasta factories opened before it was discovered that pasta was healthy.

D is incorrect because Italians grew spices in their gardens before pasta became popular and found to be healthy.

Copyright © McGraw-Hill Education

Read the passage. Then answer the questions.

Lucy Gets a Pet Sitter

I wanted to get a cute puppy more than anything else in the world. The rest of my family did not.

"Oscar is too old to enjoy an energetic puppy, Emma," said Dad. Oscar was our family's older dog.

"A puppy will chew on objects like rugs and socks, Emma," exclaimed Mom.

"I'm too busy with school and sports to pay attention to a puppy," replied my older brother James.

When my grandmother adopted a tiny puppy and named it Lucy, I found my solution. I called my grandmother on the telephone. "Grandma, I am available to take care of Lucy anytime you need me. I can be a helpful pet sitter because I can tell what a pet might need, and I love animals."

"Thank you, Emma," said Grandma. "I can't wait for you to meet Lucy."

"Oh, I can't wait either!" I cried.

GO ON →

1 Who is telling the story?

   A Dad

   B Emma

   C James

   D Grandma

2 Which statement **best** describes how the narrator feels about puppies?

   A Puppies are lovable.

   B Puppies destroy things.

   C Puppies provide company for other pets.

   D Puppies require too much time to train.

GO ON →

Read the passage. Then answer the questions.

Noah's Sled

Noah unloaded his sled into the new garage. *I won't need this in the South,* he sighed. Noah's family had moved from Michigan, and Noah had left his friends behind.

Little did he know that an unusual winter storm was about to blow in, and when Noah awoke in his new bedroom, he saw a familiar sight out the window—snow!

Even though it was predawn, he grabbed his sled from the garage and, with his parent's permission, he found a hill to ride down. *Zip, zoom!* As he headed back up the hill in the sunrise, he noticed a boy curiously watching him.

"Want to try?" Noah asked the boy.

"I don't know how to sled," replied the boy.

"Don't worry, I've had a lot of experience, so I can teach you!" replied Noah cheerfully.

GO ON →

3 Read the paragraph from the passage.

Little did he know that an <u>unusual</u> winter storm was about to blow in, and when Noah awoke in his new bedroom, he saw a familiar sight out the window—snow!

What does the word <u>unusual</u> mean?

A was common before

B will be common in the future

C is very common

D is not common

4 Read the sentence from the passage.

Even though it was <u>predawn</u>, he grabbed his sled from the garage and, with his parent's permission, he found a hill to ride down.

What does the word <u>predawn</u> show about Noah?

A He gets up very early.

B He gets up very late.

C He gets a full night's sleep.

D He does not get any sleep.

GO ON →

Read the passage. Then answer the questions.

Food for Thought

Ronelle and Deon tagged along after their father at the grocery store. Ronelle was in charge of watching her excitable little brother. Her father did not want him knocking things over or wandering off in the busy store. With cans stacked almost ceiling high and walls of boxes blocking her view, it was not an easy task.

"Dad, hey Dad," Deon said as he tugged on his father's sweater in an impatient way. "Can we buy something good to eat too?"

"Sure," his father mumbled, as he carefully inspected the label on a box of cereal, "but just be sure it's healthy for you."

"Yay!" Deon cheered and almost immediately pulled a box of Cheesy Potato Doodles from the middle of a stack. Ronelle dove to keep the top boxes from tumbling over. Then she looked at Deon.

"Don't you remember the time you ate almost a whole bag of those at Sam's birthday party? They made you sick!" she reminded him.

"Oh, right," Deon said thoughtfully. He handed the box to Ronelle, who replaced it lightly on top of the others.

In the next lane, Deon spotted bags of Crunchy Cracker Sticks piled in a pyramid. This time, just lifting the top bag caused the others to begin sliding downward on the slippery slope. Ronelle jumped into action and stopped the slide.

Now it was her turn to recall an unpleasant memory. "I ate those once," she told Deon. "They're so salty, and they made me really thirsty. I had to drink a million glasses of water afterward!"

"Oh," Deon said. He handed the bag to Ronelle, who didn't even try to put it atop the others. Instead, she leaned it on the side of the pile.

GO ON →

Then, Deon's eyes widened when he saw the frozen food section, and he darted over to it, almost knocking into a woman and her cart.

"Juicy Poparoos! Juicy Poparoos! I saw them on TV! I want them!" Deon shouted nonstop.

Ronelle took a carton out of the freezer and read the label to Deon. "The very first ingredient is sugar. In fact, Juicy Poparoos are nothing but sugar, water, and food coloring," said Ronelle.

"Do you remember the last time you went to the dentist? You had to have a cavity filled. Do you want to go through that again?"

"No," Deon said.

Then Ronelle noticed the fruit section nearby. Bunches of plump red grapes caught her eye.

"How about some grapes instead? They're naturally sweet, and juicy, too!" Ronelle suggested.

"Great!" said Deon.

"Phew!" thought Ronelle.

GO ON →

5   Read the sentence from the passage.

"Dad, hey Dad," Deon said as he tugged on his father's sweater in an <u>impatient</u> way.

What does the word <u>impatient</u> mean?

A   does not need to wait

B   is not willing to wait

C   has waited long enough

D   has never waited

6   By telling mainly about Deon's actions, what does the narrator show about Deon?

A   He knows what his family likes to eat.

B   He is in charge within the family.

C   He feels sorry for creating messes.

D   He has trouble making good decisions.

7   Read the paragraph below. Circle the word that has a prefix that means "not."

Now it was her turn to recall an unpleasant memory. "I ate those once," she told Deon. "They're so salty, and they made me really thirsty. I had to drink a million glasses of water afterward!"

GO ON →

8 Read the following chart.

Ronelle's Point of View	Deon's Point of View
Snacks should be healthy, without a lot of salt and sugar.	

Which detail completes the chart to show Deon's point of view?

A Snacks should taste good even if they are unhealthy.

B You can eat a lot of chips without feeling full.

C Fruits and vegetables are good choices for snacks.

D Snacks should always have colorful and fun labels.

9 Read the paragraph from the passage.

"Juicy Poparoos! Juicy Poparoos! I saw them on TV! I want them!" Deon shouted <u>nonstop</u>.

What does the word <u>nonstop</u> mean?

A stopping again

B before stopping

C stopping often

D without stopping

10 With which statement would Ronelle **most likely** agree?

A Everyone should eat what they want.

B Families should help one another.

C Exercise is more important than diet.

D Healthy snacks have fun names.

Answer Key

Student Name: _____

Question	Correct Answer	Content Focus	Complexity
1	B	Point of View	DOK 2
2	A	Point of View	DOK 3
3	D	Prefixes: *un-, non-, im-, pre-*	DOK 1
4	A	Prefixes: *un-, non-, im-, pre-*	DOK 1
5	B	Prefixes: *un-, non-, im-, pre-*	DOK 1
6	D	Point of View	DOK 3
7	see below	Prefixes: *un-, non-, im-, pre-*	DOK 1
8	A	Point of View	DOK 3
9	D	Prefixes: *un-, non-, im-, pre-*	DOK 1
10	B	Point of View	DOK 3

Comprehension 1, 2, 6, 8, 10	/10	%
Vocabulary 3, 4, 5, 7, 9	/10	%
Total Progress Monitoring Assessment Score	/20	%

7 Students should circle the following word in the paragraph:
   • unpleasant

Unit 4 Weeks 1–2 Rationales

1

A is incorrect because Dad is not the narrator in the story, as indicated by Emma's use of the pronoun "I," but rather Dad is introduced by Emma in her retelling of the puppy experience.

B is correct because when other characters speak to the narrator, they call her by her name, Emma.

C is incorrect because James is not the narrator of the story, as indicated by Emma's use of the pronoun "I," but rather James is introduced by Emma in her retelling of the puppy experience.

D is incorrect because Grandma is not the narrator of the story, as indicated by Emma's use of the pronoun "I," but rather Grandma is introduced by Emma in her retelling of the puppy experience.

2

A is correct because Emma states that puppies are cute and that she loves animals.

B is incorrect because it is Emma's mother who thinks a puppy would be destructive.

C is incorrect because although Emma's father thinks a puppy would be too active for their current pet, nothing suggests that Emma disagrees with him and thinks a puppy would be good company.

D is incorrect because it is James who thinks a puppy would be time-consuming.

3

A is incorrect because the prefix *un-* does not mean "before"; the prefix *pre-* means "before."

B is incorrect because the prefix *post-*, not the prefix *un-*, means "after."

C is incorrect because the prefix *un-* does not mean "very."

D is correct because the prefix *un-* means "not," so *unusual* means "not common."

4

A is correct because the prefix *pre-* means "before," so *predawn* means "before dawn."

B is incorrect because the prefix *pre-* states that Noah gets up before the sun rises.

C is incorrect because the word parts of *predawn* indicate that Noah gets up before dawn; they do not tell whether he gets a full night's sleep.

D is incorrect because although the prefix *pre-* in *predawn* shows that Noah gets up early, it does not suggest that he does not get any sleep.

5

A is incorrect because the word *impatient* includes the prefix *im-*, meaning "not," and the root word "patient," so it means "not patient."

B is correct because the prefix *im-* means "not," so *impatient* means "not patient."

C is incorrect because the prefix *im-* indicates that Deon is not patient and has not waited at all.

D is incorrect because although the prefix in *impatient* suggests that the word means "not patient," this does not mean that Deon has never waited.

6

A is incorrect because Deon's choices reflect his preferences for unhealthy foods and not what his family wants.

B is incorrect because Ronelle and Dad supervise Deon.

C is incorrect because Deon seems mostly oblivious of his antics and is never apologetic.

D is correct because Deon's actions show he knocks "things over," shouts, and consistently chooses unhealthy snacks, implying he has trouble making good decisions.

7

The word *unpleasant* has the prefix *un-*, which means "not."

8

A is correct because Deon begins his snack search with the criteria of: "Can we buy something good to eat too?"

B is incorrect because various chip choices are rejected by Ronelle, and Deon never protests by saying chips help you feel full.

C is incorrect because it is Ronelle that leads Deon to choosing a fruit as a healthy snack, so the statement expresses her point of view.

D is incorrect because Deon never explicitly says he cares about how the labels look on the snacks.

9

A is incorrect because the prefix *re-* has the meaning "again," not the prefix *non-*.

B is incorrect because the prefix *pre-* has the meaning "before," not the prefix *non-*.

C is incorrect because the prefix *non-* means "without" or "not"; it does not state that something is done often.

D is correct because the prefix *non-* means "done without," so *nonstop* means "without stopping."

10

A is incorrect because Ronelle steers Deon away from his poor food choices.

B is correct because Ronelle helps both her father and Deon by trying to make smart food choices for her brother.

C is incorrect because Ronelle focuses on diet in the passage and does not mention exercise.

D is incorrect because the unhealthy snacks that attract Deon all have the fun names.

Read the passage. Then answer the questions.

How Animals Survive in Difficult Places

The amazing camel can survive almost any set of conditions in its desert home. There are many dangers in its habitat, such as heat and lack of water. Camels are able to succeed because of their special body parts. For example, they store fat in the large hump on their back. This fat keeps them cool. As a result, they don't sweat out water as much. This adaptation is very helpful because it does not rain often in the desert. Water can be hard to find. Unbelievably, camels can go one week without drinking!

Another animal that has a special way of living in a difficult place is the penguin. Penguins live in places where it is very cold and windy. Like the camel, fat helps the penguin. Penguins' fat layers keep them from freezing. However, penguins also have other resources. For example, their feathers are short and woolly, and they can fold over each other. In days with little or no sunlight, having feathers to seal in warmth is important. They can also puff up their feathers to be toastier. Even the black color of their feathers helps because black draws in heat from the sun.

GO ON →

1   Read the diagram below.

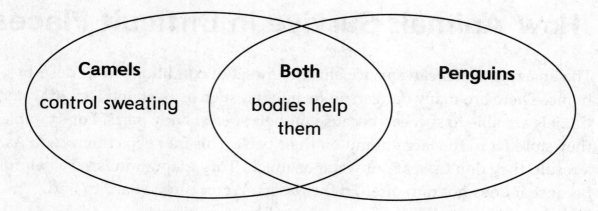

Which phrase **best** completes the diagram?

A   live in hot habitat

B   drink once a week

C   fold over feathers

D   avoid cold places

2   How are camels and penguins alike?

A   Both animals have body fat.

B   Both animals have a hump.

C   Both animals have feathers.

D   Both animals have a lot of sun.

GO ON →

Read the passage. Then answer the questions.

Is It a Leaf or An Insect?

An insect that looks like a stick or leaf can startle you because it would be hard to see in a forest of trees. Some animals use the forest as protection by changing their color. They may use camouflage, or change to match their background, as a way to hide from larger animals or seem less interesting to them. They may even change their size or shape. The trickster stick insect changes both color and shape to fool predators.

Stick insects are hard to spot among the gum trees in the forest. They can have long yellow stripes down the center of their bodies, which match the colors and patterns on gum trees. Their behavior also helps hide them because they flatten down against leaves to make themselves disappear. In fact, their body shapes look so much like leaves that they even trick other stick insects.

GO ON →

3   Read the sentence from the passage.

An insect that looks like a stick or leaf can <u>startle</u> you because it would be hard to see in a forest of trees.

What does the word <u>startle</u> mean? Use the words "hard to see" as a clue.

A bother

B grab

C surprise

D fix

4   Read the sentence from the passage.

The <u>trickster</u> stick insect changes both color and shape to fool predators.

Which word from the sentence helps the reader know the meaning of <u>trickster</u>?

A insect

B both

C shape

D fool

GO ON →

Read the passage. Then answer the questions.

Life Underwater

Do you know what life is like under the waves? A coral reef is one of the best places to go because the water is warm and there are lots of fish to see. However, few humans ever visit another part of the ocean—the deep sea. It is a cold, strange world, very different from a coral reef.

Creatures of the Sea

Coral reefs are called the rain forests of the ocean. The largest reef in the world is the massive Great Barrier Reef, which is 1,240 miles long. Billions of corals created this. Bright colors and many shapes come alive in the sunlight that shines on the reef. Coral reefs are not far from land, and sunlight allows plants and animals to live there. The reef provides a nice warm home for all kinds of living things. Animals called corals form the reef. They leave the hard part of their bodies when they die, and a large reef is made from many of these tiny body parts. Some corals form huge round shapes, or mounds, and some form shapes that look like animal horns.

The deep sea is very different from a coral reef. The deepest part of the ocean floor is mostly flat, but there are also mountains taller than any on land. There are valleys almost seven miles deep, and the water temperature is near freezing. The weight of miles and miles of water above would easily crush a car, and yet, many types of creatures are able to live there. Huge crabs, starfish, and worms survive in the deep sea.

Ocean Life Survival

On coral reefs, animals also depend on other animals and plants to live. Small fish hide from big fish in the coral. Long and thin eels wait in the holes, shooting out and grabbing a meal. Fish scrape food off the coral with their teeth. Sea grasses offer food to turtles, crabs, and fish.

GO ON →

Life on the bottom of the ocean depends on "marine snow," or tiny bits of animals and plants that sink downward from above. Giant barrel sponges six feet long eat these nonliving animals and plants. Odd animals that look like flowers also feed on this snow. There is no sunlight, so green plants cannot grow there.

Will They Have the Same Fate?

The deep ocean is very different from a coral reef. Near the ocean floor, animals survive in very cold water and without sunlight. However, ocean life everywhere might be in trouble. Coral reefs are dying off, and ocean water is getting hotter. Dirt is washing into the ocean. Perhaps only the strong creatures in the deepest and most unfriendly waters will be successful and survive.

GO ON →

Progress Monitoring Assessments

5 Read the sentence from the passage.

The largest reef in the world is the <u>massive</u> Great Barrier Reef, which is 1,240 miles long.

What does the word <u>massive</u> mean?

A huge

B dirty

C hidden

D dangerous

6 How are coral reefs and the deep sea alike?

A Both are rain forests of the ocean.

B Both are full of light.

C Both are in danger of losing ocean life.

D Both are near the ocean floor.

7 Read the sentences from the passage.

They leave the hard part of their bodies when they die, and a large <u>reef</u> is made from many of these tiny body parts. Some corals form huge round shapes, or mounds, and some form shapes that look like animal horns.

What do the words "huge round shapes" show about a <u>reef</u>?

A what it looks like

B what it sounds like

C what it smells like

D what it acts like

GO ON →

8 Complete the diagram. Write a detail from the box below in **each** section of the diagram to compare and contrast.

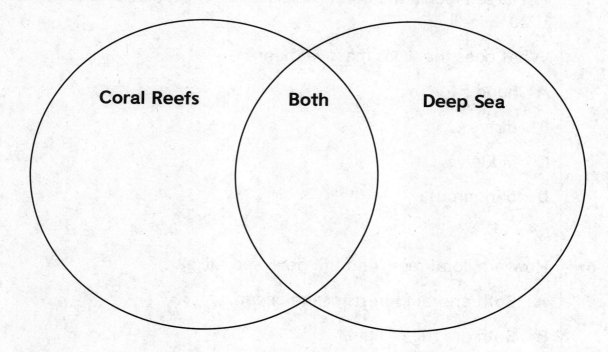

Coral Reefs   Both   Deep Sea

```
water near freezing
home for ocean life
close to land
```

GO ON →

9 Read the sentence from the passage.

Fish <u>scrape</u> food off the coral with their teeth.

Which word from the sentence helps the reader know the meaning of <u>scrape</u>?

A fish

B food

C coral

D teeth

10 How are coral reefs different from the deep sea?

A Coral reefs are growing larger.

B Coral reefs get few human visitors.

C Coral reefs have warm temperatures.

D Coral reefs include strange animals.

Answer Key

Student Name: _____

Question	Correct Answer	Content Focus	Complexity
1	C	Text Structure: Compare and Contrast	DOK 3
2	A	Text Structure: Compare and Contrast	DOK 2
3	C	Sentence Clues	DOK 2
4	D	Sentence Clues	DOK 2
5	A	Sentence Clues	DOK 2
6	C	Text Structure: Compare and Contrast	DOK 2
7	A	Sentence Clues	DOK 2
8	see below	Text Structure: Compare and Contrast	DOK 3
9	D	Sentence Clues	DOK 2
10	C	Text Structure: Compare and Contrast	DOK 2

Comprehension 1, 2, 6, 8, 10	/10	%
Vocabulary 3, 4, 5, 7, 9	/10	%
Total Progress Monitoring Assessment Score	/20	%

8   Students should complete the diagram with the following details:
- Coral Reefs: close to land
- Deep Sea: water near freezing
- Both: home for ocean life

Unit 4 Weeks 3–4 Rationales

1

A is incorrect because penguins live "in places where it is very cold," not where it is hot.

B is incorrect because camels can go without drinking for a week, but penguins cannot.

C is correct because penguins have "feathers to seal in warmth."

D is incorrect because penguins live "in places where it is very cold," so they cannot avoid the cold.

2

A is correct because both animals use body fat to survive.

B is incorrect because penguins do not have humps.

C is incorrect because camels do not have feathers.

D is incorrect because the passage mentions days of "little or no sunlight" for penguins.

3

A is incorrect because the fact that the insect is hard to see does not suggest that it would bother or annoy you.

B is incorrect because being hard to see does not indicate that the insect would grab you.

C is correct because the insect would surprise you if it were hard to see in the forest.

D is incorrect because the insect would not fix anything simply because it is hard to see.

4

A is incorrect because the word *insect* alone does not give a clue to the meaning of *trickster*.

B is incorrect because the word *both* does not give a clue to the meaning of *trickster*.

C is incorrect because the word *shape* is part of the idea that the insect stays safe, which does not provide a direct clue to what *trickster* means.

D is correct because the word *fool* provides a direct clue to what *trickster* means and what a *trickster* does.

5

A is correct because the sentence clue *largest* hints that *massive* means "huge."

B is incorrect because clues in the sentence suggest that the Great Barrier Reef is big, not dirty.

C is incorrect because there are no context clues that hint that the Great Barrier Reef is hidden.

D is incorrect because the Great Barrier Reef is described as "the largest reef in the world," which means that it is huge, not dangerous.

6

A is incorrect because only coral reefs are called the rain forests of the ocean.

B is incorrect because only the coral reef has sunlight.

C is correct because ocean life in both the coral reefs and the deep sea "might be in trouble."

D is incorrect because only the deep sea is located at the bottom of the ocean.

7

A is correct because the description explains what a coral reef looks like.

B is incorrect because "huge round shapes" does not suggest how the coral reef sounds.

C is incorrect because "huge round shapes" does not suggest what the coral reef smells like.

D is incorrect because the reader cannot know how a reef might act like based only on its shape.

8

The passage explains that coral reefs exist close to land, while the deep sea does not. It also describes how the water is near freezing only in the deep sea. However, both are a home for ocean life.

9

A is incorrect because the fact that fish are performing the action does not explain what the action is.

B is incorrect because *food* tells what is receiving the action, but not what the action is.

C is incorrect because *coral* is related to the action of scraping, but it does not explain what is happening.

D is correct because *teeth* is a clue that *scrape* means "to cut or remove with a sharp implement."

10

A is incorrect because coral reefs are not growing larger, and the deep sea isn't said to be growing.

B is incorrect because people visit coral reefs instead of the deep sea.

C is correct because details support that coral reefs are warm and sunny while the deep sea is cold and dark.

D is incorrect because the deep sea is described as a "strange world."

Read the poem. Then answer the questions.

More Than Mashed Potatoes

I used to hate art class
'Til my teacher helped me see
That what my eyes are seeing
Are not what things can be.

5   Mashed potatoes aren't potatoes,
That's what he said to me.
"They're a mountain. They're a cloud.
Pour some gravy. Make a sea."

A block of wood is just that—
10   A piece of wood, I say.
My teacher tells me, "Look again.
Here's a tool. Go carve away."

Now a block of wood it's not,
It's a spaceship or a car.
15   Just remove some extra wood,
Teacher, look! I am a star!

Water paints aren't only colors,
They become just what you wish.
With some paper, brush, and water
20   I create a deep-sea fish.

Now wire's not just metal,
It's a thin man or a cat.
Make a silly face or tree
Bend it this way, or like that.

GO ON →

25   Sticks and stones, feathers, shells,
Each is much more than what you see.
And I—master cook—make art with them,
Following my recipe.

I understand art better now
30   Even though I'm not the smartest
There is one thing I'm certain of—
I am QUITE the artist.

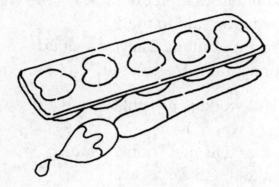

GO ON →

1 What lesson does the student learn in this poem?

    A Working together achieves success.

    B Ability is necessary for artistic talent.

    C Making quick decisions brings results.

    D Using imagination opens possibilities.

2 Read the lines from the poem.

Now a block of wood it's not,
It's a spaceship or a car.
Just remove some extra wood,
Teacher, look! I am a star!

What is a block of wood being compared to?

    A a spaceship

    B extra wood

    C the teacher

    D a star

GO ON →

3 Write a check next to **three** lines that support the theme of the poem.

☐	Are not what things can be. (line 4)
☐	A block of wood is just that— (line 9)
☐	A piece of wood, I say. (line 10)
☐	They become just what you wish. (line 18)
☐	Each is much more than what you see. (line 26)

4 Read the lines from the poem.

Sticks and stones, feathers, shells,
Each is much more than what you see.
And I—master cook—make art with them,
Following my recipe.

What do the words "master cook" show about the speaker?

A The speaker oversees others.

B The speaker manages a kitchen.

C The speaker works at the highest level.

D The speaker uses materials to create.

GO ON →

5 What is the main message of the poem?

   A Being helpful to others can bring joy.

   B Sometimes things are more than what they seem to be.

   C Trying something new can bring big mistakes.

   D People often know more than they think they do.

Answer Key

Student Name: _____

Question	Correct Answer	Content Focus	Complexity
1	D	Theme	DOK 3
2	A	Metaphor	DOK 2
3	see below	Theme	DOK 3
4	D	Metaphor	DOK 2
5	B	Theme	DOK 3

Comprehension 1, 3, 5	/6	%
Vocabulary 2, 4	/4	%
Total Progress Monitoring Assessment Score	/10	%

3 Students should check the boxes for the following lines from the poem:

- Are not what things can be. (line 4)
- They become just what you wish. (line 18)
- Each is much more than what you see. (line 26)

Unit 4 Week 5 Rationales

1

A is incorrect because the young artist achieves success individually with some guidance.

B is incorrect because the young artist is just learning what his abilities are.

C is incorrect because the young artist begins looking carefully at materials, not quickly.

D is correct because the artist learns of materials that "each is more than what you see."

2

A is correct because a metaphor compares two different things without using the words *like* or *as*. The block of wood is not just that, but "it's a spaceship."

B is incorrect because the metaphor is not comparing the block of wood to extra wood.

C is incorrect because the metaphor is not comparing the block of wood to the teacher.

D is incorrect because the metaphor is not comparing the block of wood to a star. The star is a metaphor for the narrator.

3

These three lines support the theme of using one's imagination:

Are not what things can be. (line 4)

They become just what you wish. (line 18)

Each is much more than what you see. (line 26)

4

A is incorrect because this detail misses the comparison in the metaphor by applying only to a master cook.

B is incorrect because this detail misses the comparison in the metaphor by applying only to a master cook.

C is incorrect because this detail misses the comparison in the metaphor by applying only to a master cook.

D is correct because the metaphor compares an artist to a cook because both use raw materials to create.

5

A is incorrect because the young artist achieves success individually, and the teacher's emotions about the student's work are unknown.

B is correct because the artist learns that for the materials, "each is more than what you see."

C is incorrect because the artist learns to work with materials in a new way and finds that things are unexpected but does not mention mistakes.

D is incorrect because the young artist begins looking carefully at materials to gain a new perspective, not to validate current knowledge.

Read the passage. Then answer the questions.

Beatrix Potter: Lover of Nature

Beatrix Potter was born on July 28, 1866. She lived in a large house in London, England, where she was educated at home.

During the summers, Beatrix Potter and her family went to stay in a country house. Potter loved to explore the forests and meadows. She had rabbits, a snake, a frog, and two lizards. Potter observed and sketched the animals. She even named the rabbits Peter Piper and Benjamin Bouncer.

Later, when Potter was an adult, she wrote a letter to a five-year-old child. He was sick at the time. To cheer him up, she drew pictures of her childhood rabbits. She also wrote a story about them. The story was such a success that Potter went on to write a collection of short stories in a book titled *The Tale of Peter Rabbit*. Potter wrote other books and became a famous author. In all, Beatrix Potter wrote 22 excellent books for children.

Potter loved the country. She wanted to protect it, so she bought many acres of land with lakes and forests. She died in 1943, but she left her farms and land to the government. Today, this land is still protected because of her. Now, everyone can enjoy nature and the animals she loved.

GO ON →

1 Which sentence **best** describes the author's point of view about the country?

   A It was too quiet for Potter.

   B It was important to Potter.

   C It made Potter feel like she was alone.

   D It taught Potter everything she knew.

2 Which sentence from the passage **best** states what the author thinks about Beatrix Potter?

   A "Potter loved to explore the forests and meadows."

   B "Later, when Potter was an adult, she wrote a letter to a five-year-old child."

   C "In all, Beatrix Potter wrote 22 excellent books for children."

   D "She died in 1943, but she left her farms and land to the government."

GO ON →

Read the passage. Then answer the questions.

Sarah Breedlove: Inspiring Business Owner

Sarah Breedlove went from being a washerwoman to making a fortune selling hair products. Her company provided jobs to thousands of African-American women, and her employees were able to improve the lives in their communities.

Breedlove was born in 1867. As a child, she worked alongside her parents picking cotton. Unhappy with this life, she moved to St. Louis where her brothers lived and became a washerwoman.

One day, Breedlove ordered a product that was made to grow hair, and she loved it. Her hair looked healthy and shiny. She decided to sell hair products, and she took them all around the country.

Breedlove was successful at business. She trained women in her haircare methods. She earned money, and so did the women who sold her products. She became one of the richest business owners in America. Before she died, Breedlove encouraged her employees to use their experience to improve their communities. They could fight for rights for all people. Not only was Breedlove a good business owner, but she was a good citizen, too.

GO ON →

3   Read the sentence from the passage.

<u>Unhappy</u> with this life, she moved to St. Louis where her brothers lived and became a washerwoman.

What does the word <u>unhappy</u> mean?

A very happy

B happy again

C happy before

D not happy

4   Read the sentence from the passage.

Breedlove was <u>successful</u> at business.

What does the word <u>successful</u> mean?

A full of success

B without success

C making success

D too much success

GO ON →

Read the passage. Then answer the questions.

Garrett Morgan: Stopping Traffic

Garrett Morgan was born in 1877 in Paris, Kentucky. His parents were former slaves. He grew up on a farm, but Morgan knew that farm life was not for him. He left the farm when he was a teenager to seek better opportunities.

In 1895, Morgan moved to Cleveland, Ohio, where he found a job fixing sewing machines. He loved finding new ways to make the machines better, and the news of his skills traveled fast.

In 1907, Morgan opened his own sewing equipment and repair shop, and soon his business shot up. It was time to expand, so, in 1909, he opened his own tailoring shop that sold coats, suits and dresses. Everything was sewn with the machines he had made himself. As the years went by, Morgan's success grew, and so did people's respect for him. He became an important person in the city of Cleveland.

Morgan thought nothing was impossible. He was always thinking about what he could do next. He invented many things. In 1912, he invented a gas mask, which he called a safety hood. It allowed people to breathe clean air when there was a lot of smoke. He thought it would help firefighters do their job.

In 1916, Morgan used his invention when there was an explosion that trapped workers who were building a tunnel underground. There was a lot of smoke. Morgan and a team of volunteers used his gas masks to help save some of the workers. Morgan later received requests from fire departments that wanted to purchase the gas masks. His gas mask was later updated for use by the U.S. Army. The U.S. soldiers used them during the First World War. Morgan won a gold medal for the invention of his gas mask.

GO ON →

During this time, the streets of Cleveland were very busy. It was common for bicycles, horse-pulled wagons, and cars to share the same streets. There were some traffic signals on the streets, but they had only two signals: stop and go. This was not the only problem. Someone had to change the signal from stop to go by hand. If the person forgot to change the signal, there were accidents. Also, there was no time between stop and go, which caused a lot of accidents, too.

One day, Morgan saw a bad accident: an automobile hit a horse and carriage. As a result, he wisely decided that he would make the streets as safe as he could. He invented a new type of traffic signal, a T-shaped pole that had three signals. The first signal was *stop,* the second signal was *go,* and the third signal stopped traffic all ways. It made all the cars, carts, and horses stop for a few seconds. Then it changed to go for some of the traffic. That made it safer for drivers. It also allowed people to cross busy streets safely. He received a patent for the signal in 1923.

The amount of traffic we have now is greater than it was in Morgan's time. However, we can still see his type of traffic signal helping to make the streets safe. Morgan would probably be proud of his invention if he saw how it worked today.

GO ON →

5   Read the sentence from the passage.

Morgan thought nothing was <u>impossible</u>.

What does the word <u>impossible</u> mean?

A   the opposite of possible

B   possible only sometimes

C   able to make possible

D   the act of being possible

6   What is the author's point of view about Garrett Morgan?

A   He did not invent enough things.

B   He had old-fashioned ideas.

C   He was talented and creative.

D   He was the greatest inventor in history.

GO ON →

7   Read the sentence from the passage.

It also allowed people to cross busy streets <u>safely</u>.

What does the word <u>safely</u> tell about how people crossed the street?

A   in a safe way

B   with someone else who was safe

C   without remembering to be safe

D   before being safe

8   Underline **two** sentences from the passage that show the author's point of view.

"He left the farm when he was a teenager to seek better opportunities."

"In 1912, he invented a gas mask, which he called a safety hood."

"Morgan won a gold medal for the invention of his gas mask."

"As a result, he wisely decided that he would make the streets as safe as he could."

"Morgan would probably be proud of his invention if he saw how it worked today."

GO ON →

9 Read the sentence from the passage.

The amount of traffic we have now is <u>greater</u> than it was in Morgan's time.

Using the suffix *-er*, what does the word <u>greater</u> mean?

A again

B more

C most

D not

10 With which statement would the author **most likely** agree?

A Success causes others to doubt you.

B Success mainly has to do with being lucky.

C Success is connected to how hard you work.

D Success is related to how much money you have.

Progress Monitoring Assessments

Answer Key

Student Name: _____

Question	Correct Answer	Content Focus	Complexity
1	B	Author's Point of View	DOK 3
2	C	Author's Point of View	DOK 2
3	D	Prefixes and Suffixes	DOK 1
4	A	Prefixes and Suffixes	DOK 1
5	A	Prefixes and Suffixes	DOK 1
6	C	Author's Point of View	DOK 3
7	A	Prefixes and Suffixes	DOK 1
8	see below	Author's Point of View	DOK 2
9	B	Prefixes and Suffixes	DOK 1
10	C	Author's Point of View	DOK 3

Comprehension 1, 2, 6, 8, 10	/10	%
Vocabulary 3, 4, 5, 7, 9	/10	%
Total Progress Monitoring Assessment Score	/20	%

8 Students should underline the following sentences:
- "As a result, he wisely decided that he would make the streets as safe as he could."
- "Morgan would probably be proud of his invention if he saw how it worked today."

Unit 5 Weeks 1–2 Rationales

1

A is incorrect because details in the passage show that Potter preferred the country and did not find it too quiet.

B is correct because details show that Potter preferred the country and wanted to protect it.

C is incorrect because there is nothing in the passage to indicate that Potter felt alone because she was in the country.

D is incorrect because nothing in the passage suggests that the country taught Potter everything she knew.

2

A is incorrect because this sentence provides a detail about Potter but does not give the author's opinion.

B is incorrect because this detail tells a fact and not an opinion.

C is correct because this detail includes the word *excellent*, which indicates that the author has a high opinion of Potter as a writer.

D is incorrect because this detail tells only what Potter did and not what the author thinks about it.

3

A is incorrect because the prefix *un-* means "not or the opposite of," rather than "very."

B is incorrect because the prefix *un-* means "not or the opposite of," rather than "again."

C is incorrect because the prefix *un-* means "not or the opposite of," rather than "before."

D is correct because *unhappy* means "not happy" or "the opposite of happy."

4

A is correct because *successful* means "full of or characterized by success."

B is incorrect because the suffix *-ful* means "full of or characterized by," rather than "without."

C is incorrect because the suffix *-ful* means "full of or characterized by," rather than "making."

D is incorrect because the suffix *-ful* means "full of or characterized by," rather than "too much."

5

A is correct because the prefix *im-* means "the opposite of," so *impossible* means "the opposite of possible."

B is incorrect because the prefix *im-* does not mean "sometimes."

C is incorrect because the prefix *im-* does not mean "able to make."

D is incorrect because the prefix *im-* does not mean "the act of."

6

A is incorrect because the author does not indicate that Morgan did not have enough inventions.

B is incorrect because the author explains how Morgan's inventions were innovative for the time period.

C is correct because the author discusses how Morgan was able to solve problems in new and creative ways.

D is incorrect because the author does not give an opinion about how important Morgan was in relation to other inventors in history.

7

A is correct because the suffix *-ly* means "like" or "characteristic of," so *safely* means "in a safe way."

B is incorrect because the suffix *-ly* does not mean "someone who is."

C is incorrect because the suffix *-ly* does not mean "remembering to be."

D is incorrect because the suffix *-ly* does not mean "before."

8

Students should underline the following sentences because they include the word *wisely* and the words *would probably be proud*:

"As a result, he wisely decided that he would make the streets as safe as he could."

"Morgan would probably be proud of his invention if he saw how it worked today."

9

A is incorrect because the prefix *re-* means "again."

B is correct because the suffix *-er* means "more."

C is incorrect because the suffix *-est* means "most."

D is incorrect because certain prefixes mean "not," not suffixes.

10

A is incorrect because the details in the passage do not support this point of view.

B is incorrect because the details in the passage do not support this point of view.

C is correct because the author indicates that Morgan worked hard to solve many problems with his inventions.

D is incorrect because the details in the passage do not support this point of view.

Read the passage. Then answer the questions.

The Magic Waterfall

Once upon a time, a woodcutter split logs with his son. The father worked all day in the heat of the forest.

"I'm so hot," said the woodcutter, "that all I can think of is a nice cool drink of water."

The son said to himself, "If only I could get some icy water for my father so that he feels refreshed."

Then, the sound of water caught his ear, and he followed the noise to a beautiful waterfall. He cupped his hands and drank the cool, clear water. To his amazement, he felt magically energized.

Overjoyed, he filled his gourd and presented the water to his grateful father. After drinking the water, the father was able to work better than ever.

News spread throughout the village of the magical water, and soon all the villagers were pushing their way up to the waterfall.

"We've been tricked!" the villagers cried. "This water is cold, but we don't feel stronger." Upset, they returned to their homes.

Glad to have avoided their anger, the boy put some water to his lips. To his astonishment, he again felt restored and stronger than ever. It seemed the waterfall produced magical water for the good son and father, but for all others, it was only ordinary.

GO ON →

1 Who is telling the story?

    A a villager from the town

    B the woodcutter

    C the woodcutter's son

    D a narrator that is not a character

2 Read the following chart.

Son's Point of View	Villagers' Point of View
Finding the water can help my father.	

Which detail belongs in the blank to show the villagers' point of view of the water?

    A Drinking the water can help us be strong.

    B Drinking the water can help us be rich.

    C Drinking the water can make us thirsty.

    D Drinking the water can make us clever.

GO ON →

Read the passage. Then answer the questions.

The Crow's Quill

There was once a young girl named Anabelle who did not have a family to take care of her. Anabelle worked as a cook in a castle, but she was not very good at her job. She often burnt the food and was laughed at by the other servants.

One day, a crow appeared at the kitchen window and spoke to Anabelle. "Pull out one of my feathers and write down a wish," it said, "and whatever you wish for will come true."

Anabelle's only wish was to be good at her work so that she had a safe place to stay. She worried that she would lose her position in the castle as a cook. Carefully, she pulled out the quill and then wrote the name of the finest, most delicious dish she could imagine. Suddenly, the food appeared on the dining table in polished, sparkling bowls, and everyone stood in awe, their mouths watering at the sight of such a meal.

The prince, who happened to be in the dining hall that day, was thrilled at the sight, too. With one taste, he fell in love with Anabelle's cooking. Anabelle smiled, relieved to know that her place at the castle had been secured.

GO ON →

3 Read the sentence from the passage.

She <u>worried</u> that she would lose her position in the castle as a cook.

What is the root word of <u>worried</u>?

A worrying

B worry

C or

D ed

4 Read the sentence from the passage.

Suddenly, the food appeared on the dining table in polished, <u>sparkling</u> bowls, and everyone stood in awe, their mouths watering at the sight of such a meal.

What does the root word of <u>sparkling</u> mean?

A fight

B find

C shine

D keep

GO ON →

Read the passage. Then answer the questions.

The Boy and the Cat
A European Fairy Tale

Once upon a time, a miller in the town of Carabas left his property to his three sons. All the riches he had were his mill, his donkey, and his cat. He gave one item to each son. The youngest son was unhappy to receive only a cat.

"My brothers can use their gifts to make a small fortune, but I will starve with just a cat," the boy complained. Meanwhile, the cat heard his new master. He wanted to please the young man, who seemed so upset.

"Please, Master, just get me a bag and some boots," requested the cat. The young man did not think the request was too strange, as he had seen the clever cat play tricks to catch a meal. And so, he gave the cat the bag and boots.

The cat looked very fancy in the boots and with the bag around his neck. "He is indeed a Puss in Boots!" smiled the boy.

Puss dashed away to catch some rats, shouting, "If you will trust me, we will come through this hardship!" Then he disappeared into the brambles, where there were a great number of rats. The cat placed some bran into his bag and stretched out as if he were asleep. The rats crawled into the bag for the snacks he had put inside of it.

But instead of taking his catch to his master, Puss went straight to a wealthy Ogre's castle. "I have brought you a rabbit, sir," the cat lied to the Ogre. "It's a gift from my master, the Master of Carabas."

"Who?" asked the Ogre, who was never quick to trust others because they were always after his riches.

GO ON →

"That doesn't matter," said Puss quickly. "I am a servant of the Master of Carabas. He has sent me to present this gift and to catch your rats," said the cat.

"What rats?" asked the Ogre. The cat brushed past the giant and rushed about the castle with a *meow* and *clatter*. He returned with his bag full of rats that he had entered with. The giant was unaware that the rats had been in the bag all along and there never was a rabbit.

The Ogre was very impressed with the rats in the bag. "I did not realize I had so many rats!" he thought. He decided he needed the cat's services and told Puss to stay and live at the castle.

"Oh, that's impossible, as the Master of Carabas will want me back," said Puss with an innocent look.

This angered the Ogre, who was used to getting what he wanted. So, Puss suggested that the boy come to live at the castle, as well.

The boy and the cat lived together very well after that in the splendid castle. They became the best of friends and had many adventures together. Meanwhile, the Ogre bragged to his neighbors about his incredible, rat-catching Puss in Boots!

GO ON →

5   What is the cat's point of view about his master?

     A   He cares for his master.

     B   He finds his master funny.

     C   He hopes to teach his master.

     D   He wants to get a new master.

6   Read the sentence from the passage.

Then he <u>disappeared</u> into the brambles, where there were a great number of rats.

What is the root word of <u>disappeared</u>?

     A   dis

     B   appear

     C   eared

     D   ed

7   Read the paragraph below. Underline the word that has a root meaning "riches."

But instead of taking his catch to his master, Puss went straight to a wealthy Ogre's castle. "I have brought you a rabbit, sir," the cat lied to the Ogre. "It's a gift from my master, the Master of Carabas."

GO ON →

8   Read the following chart.

Ogre's Point of View	Boy's Point of View
	The cat cannot help me.

Which detail belongs in the blank to show the Ogre's point of view?

A   The cat is annoying.

B   The cat is a good friend.

C   The cat is a great help.

D   The cat is causing problems.

9   Read the sentence from the passage.

"I am a <u>servant</u> of the Master of Carabas."

What does the root of the word <u>servant</u> mean?

A   cut

B   eat

C   assist

D   leave

10   By telling mainly about the cat's actions, what does the narrator show about the cat?

A   The cat gets scared easily.

B   The cat solves problems in clever ways.

C   The cat has little experience with the world.

D   The cat does not like challenges.

Answer Key

Student Name: _____

Question	Correct Answer	Content Focus	Complexity
1	D	Point of View	DOK 2
2	A	Point of View	DOK 3
3	B	Root Words	DOK 1
4	C	Root Words	DOK 1
5	A	Point of View	DOK 3
6	B	Root Words	DOK 1
7	see below	Root Words	DOK 1
8	C	Point of View	DOK 3
9	C	Root Words	DOK 1
10	B	Point of View	DOK 3

Comprehension 1, 2, 5, 8, 10	/10	%
Vocabulary 3, 4, 6, 7, 9	/10	%
Total Progress Monitoring Assessment Score	/20	%

7   Students should underline the following word in the paragraph:
  • wealthy

Unit 5 Weeks 3–4 Rationales

1

A is incorrect because the story is not written from a first-person point of view.

B is incorrect because the story is not written from a first-person point of view.

C is incorrect because the story is not written from a first-person point of view.

D is correct because the story is written from a third-person point of view.

2

A is correct because details show the villagers want to help themselves be strong and not someone else.

B is incorrect because details show that the villagers are not concerned about being rich.

C is incorrect because nothing suggests that the villagers think they will be thirsty as a result of drinking the water.

D is incorrect because nothing suggests that the villagers think they will be clever as a result of drinking the water.

3

A is incorrect because *worrying* is another word that uses the same root word as *worried*.

B is correct because *worry* and the suffix *-ed* are used to create the word *worried*.

C is incorrect because these letters are not a word part in *worried*.

D is incorrect because this is the suffix in *worried*.

4

A is incorrect because *sparkling* does not mean "to fight."

B is incorrect because *sparkling* does not mean "to find."

C is correct because *sparkle* is the root word of *sparkling*, which means "to shine."

D is incorrect because *sparkling* does not mean "to keep."

5

A is correct because the second paragraph says that the cat wants to please his new master.

B is incorrect because the cat does not indicate that he finds his new master funny.

C is incorrect because the cat does not indicate that he hopes to teach his new master something.

D is incorrect because the cat does not indicate that he wants to leave his master.

6

A is incorrect because *dis-* is a prefix of *disappeared*; it is not the root word.

B is correct because *appear* is the root word of *disappeared*.

C is incorrect because *eared* is not the root word of *disappeared*.

D is incorrect because *-ed* is a suffix of *disappeared*; it is not the root word.

7

Students should underline the word *wealthy* because it includes the root word *wealth,* which means "riches."

8

A is incorrect because the Ogre is initially distrustful of the cat but does not say he's annoying.

B is incorrect because the Ogre wants the cat to catch rats, not to be his friend.

C is correct because the Ogre thinks the cat has caught a lot of rats in the castle.

D is incorrect because the Ogre believes that the cat is solving problems by catching rats.

9

A is incorrect because the root word of *servant* is *serve,* which does not mean "cut."

B is incorrect because the root word of *servant* is *serve,* which does not mean "eat."

C is correct because the root word of *servant* is *serve,* which means "assist."

D is incorrect because the root word of *servant* is *serve,* which does not mean "leave."

10

A is incorrect because although the Ogre could be scary, the cat handles the Ogre bravely.

B is correct because the narrator focuses on the cat's clever problem solving.

C is incorrect because it is the boy who is inexperienced and cannot solve his own problems.

D is incorrect because it is the boy who becomes discouraged when faced with a challenge.

Read the passage. Then answer the questions.

Electric Cars: The Future Is Now!

These days, many people want to "go green." They know that burning gasoline causes pollution. Because of this, more people should be driving electric cars.

The electric car is not a new invention. In fact, this great technology has been around since the 1880s. Here is how electric cars work. They have large, powerful batteries that send electricity to an electric motor. The motor turns the wheels. When the batteries run low on energy, they must be plugged in to recharge.

Electric cars are very special. For one thing, they don't use gasoline. Today, the cost of gas continues to rise. More people are concerned about pollution, as well. An electric car costs a small amount of money to recharge, and it also produces almost no pollution. That's why more electric car models are offered for sale every year and why more people should be buying them!

Some people don't like electric cars. They say that an electric car is a "neighborhood car" because it cannot travel long distances without needing to be charged. However, this is not true. Some of the better cars can last for more than 200 miles before they need to be charged and because cars are improving every year, this number will only go up! Knowing this information should encourage more people to drive electric cars.

Another great thing about electric cars is that they can be recharged using any electrical outlet. Drivers can even run an extension cord from their house to their car. Charging stations have been built in some cities, as well. Recharging is much faster at one of these stations. There should be no excuse to not buy an electric car.

GO ON →

Electric cars have other benefits, too. They run very quietly, and they also cost less than regular cars to maintain. That is because they have fewer parts. Batteries have to be replaced only once every 10–15 years. Less maintenance should mean more electric cars on the road!

There are a lot of reasons why electric cars are the best choice. They don't use gasoline. That means they help you save money. They are also good for the environment. They are easy to recharge, and they are very quiet. Finally, they do not require as many repairs. So why aren't more electric cars on the road? That is a good question! Maybe people don't know enough about electric cars. That should change. People think of electric cars as the cars of the future, but the future is now! It's time to get out of your old car and into an electric one!

GO ON →

Progress Monitoring Assessments

1   Why are electric cars good for the environment?

     A   They are quiet to operate.

     B   They are easy to recharge.

     C   They do not create pollution.

     D   They do not need many repairs.

2   Read the sentence from the passage.

     The electric car is not a <u>new</u> invention.

     What does the word <u>new</u> mean?

     A   a letter in an alphabet

     B   a type of animal

     C   past tense of being aware

     D   made a short time ago

GO ON →

3 Read the diagram below.

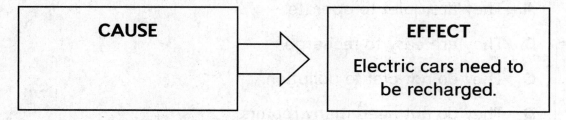

CAUSE		EFFECT
	→	Electric cars need to be recharged.

Which sentence **best** completes the diagram?

A Batteries get low on energy.

B Charging stations are only in some locations.

C People with electric cars save money on gasoline.

D Electric cars have fewer parts than other types of cars.

4 Read the sentence from the passage.

That's why more electric car models are offered for <u>sale</u> every year and why more people should be buying them!

What does the word <u>sale</u> mean?

A made available to buy

B a lower price

C fabric that uses wind to move

D to travel over water

GO ON →

5 Write the statement that describes the effect of **each** cause. Use the statements from the box below.

Cause	**Effect**
Cause 1: Electricity runs an electric car's motor.	
Cause 2: Some electric cars go 200 miles on one charge.	

Statements

People with electric cars can travel long distances.

People with electric cars can use a battery rather than gasoline.

STOP

Answer Key

Student Name: _____

Question	Correct Answer	Content Focus	Complexity
1	C	Cause and Effect	DOK 2
2	D	Context Clues: Homophones	DOK 1
3	A	Cause and Effect	DOK 2
4	A	Context Clues: Homophones	DOK 1
5	see below	Cause and Effect	DOK 2

Comprehension 1, 3, 5	/6	%
Vocabulary 2, 4	/4	%
Total Progress Monitoring Assessment Score	/10	%

5   Students should complete the diagram with the following statements:

- Cause 1—Effect: People with electric cars can use a battery rather than gasoline.
- Cause 2—Effect: People with electric cars can travel long distances.

Unit 5 Week 5 Rationales

1

A is incorrect because the effect of being quiet is mostly a benefit to drivers and not the environment.

B is incorrect because the effect of being easy to recharge is mostly a benefit to drivers and not the environment.

C is correct because the effect of running on a battery is that electric cars do not produce pollution.

D is incorrect because the effect of making fewer repairs is mostly a benefit to drivers and not the environment.

2

A is incorrect because *nu* is a homophone that means "a letter in the Greek alphabet."

B is incorrect because *gnu* is a homophone that means "an African antelope."

C is incorrect because *knew* is a homophone that means "past tense of know"

D is correct because *new* means "having been made a short time ago."

3

A is correct because the effect of a low battery is that it requires recharging.

B is incorrect because the location of charging stations does not cause cars to need to be recharged.

C is incorrect because the cause of a battery recharge isn't saving money; that is an effect of using a battery versus gasoline.

D is incorrect because the effect of having fewer parts is saving money, not recharging.

4

A is correct because the car models are made available to buy.

B is incorrect because this is an alternate meaning of *sale*.

C is incorrect because this is a meaning of the homophone *sail*.

D is incorrect because this is a meaning of the homophone *sail*.

5

Students should complete the chart with the following statements:

Cause 1—Effect: People with electric cars can use a battery rather than gasoline.

Cause 2— Effect: People with electric cars can travel long distances.

Read the passage. Then answer the questions.

Alvin McDonald and Wind Cave

As a young boy, Alvin McDonald was captivated by a special cave. From the moment he entered Wind Cave, he decided on a life of exploration and adventure. There were few tools for exploring. So, for several years, young McDonald lit a candle and rolled out a string to mark his way through the cave.

We know about his love for Wind Cave because, when he was just about 18 years old, McDonald started writing about the cave in a journal. He described finding strange fossils and purple crystals. Eventually, McDonald became a tour guide. He helped visitors learn more about Wind Cave.

McDonald enjoyed taking visitors around the cave. He even called himself its "chief guide." Whenever he was away, he claimed he felt homesick for it and wanted to return. After three years of exploring, he admitted that the cave was a complex system and he would never find all of its tunnels and passageways. When McDonald died, he was buried near the cave entrance. A bronze sign helps us remember his great love for Wind Cave.

GO ON →

1   Read the diagram below.

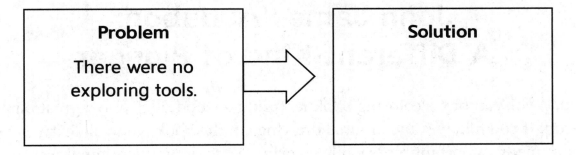

Which sentence **best** completes the diagram?

A   McDonald found purple crystals.

B   McDonald became a tour guide for the cave.

C   McDonald marked his way with string.

D   McDonald wrote about the cave in a journal.

2   What problem did McDonald have when he was away from Wind Cave?

A   No one visited it.

B   He missed it.

C   He got lost in it.

D   No one took care of it.

GO ON →

Read the passage. Then answer the questions.

John James Audubon: A Different Kind of Pioneer

Today, you can buy a coloring book featuring a wood duck and a great blue heron. If you follow some original drawings in the book, you will learn about many important birds while coloring. Who drew the original pictures? The artist is John James Audubon. He's known as America's most famous painter-naturalist. A naturalist is a person who studies plants and animals.

Audubon lived on America's wild lands, but he was a different kind of pioneer. His work was one of both artist and scientist because he painted birds in their natural surroundings. Was he good at art? At first, his sketches were rather lifeless, but Audubon got better and began using watercolors. He took care to paint each bird's special features, and he showed how each bird lived. He did this by including flowers, berries, or the bird's predators.

Eventually, Audubon published a book of his drawings. It took a long time to make that happen. *The Birds of America* became a famous book and is still well-known today. Audubon used his skills to teach people about the life histories of nearly 500 kinds of birds.

GO ON →

3   Read the sentence from the passage.

Who drew the <u>original</u> pictures?

The word <u>original</u> comes from a Latin word that means "source of something." What does the word <u>original</u> mean?

A   largest

B   newest

C   best

D   first

4   Read the sentence from the passage.

A naturalist is a person who <u>studies</u> plants and animals.

The word <u>studies</u> comes from a Latin word that means "to be busy with." What does <u>studies</u> mean?

A   learns about something

B   forgets about something

C   rests the mind

D   rests the body

GO ON →

Read the passage. Then answer the questions.

Nellie Bly: Making a Difference

As a young girl, Nellie Bly was nicknamed "Pinky" because she wore pink dresses. This was not the only special thing about her, though. She also set her sights on other interests. During the late 1860s, Bly was smart and determined enough to dream of teaching. But despite having to leave school for lack of money, that didn't stop Bly from doing big things.

The Letter

At age 16, an article changed Bly's life. The article upset her because it questioned the importance of girls. But what could Bly do? She wrote a response to the newspaper, and it was so well-written and interesting that the editor offered Bly a job.

New Challenges

Bly wanted to be a journalist who wrote about important issues. She tried hard to get the facts for her stories. Sometimes she had to bravely go undercover to search for answers. For example, she went into a hospital as a patient and wrote about the bad conditions there. When her article was published, the hospital had to make improvements. Bly knew the dangers of her job, but she continued writing about bad conditions in different industries in order to help others. People couldn't wait to read her articles!

Setting a Record

Then, one day Bly had the idea of breaking a record by racing around the world in less than 80 days. Along the way, people cheered for her exciting trip, and, of course, she kept notes about interesting places she visited, such as Japan and the Suez Canal.

GO ON →

Everything didn't go smoothly, though. A huge snowstorm caused delays. She also had competition from another reporter. But Bly found ways to keep to her schedule, and she made it around the world in just 72 days. The other reporter arrived four days later. Bly had won the race! The now-famous reporter wrote about her record-breaking, worldwide adventure in *Nellie Bly's Book: Around the World in Seventy-Two Days*. Soon, her picture was on trading cards, board games, and other products.

Why Stop There?

By now, Bly had been writing about what she wanted for quite a while. In her 30s, she decided on a new career by becoming an inventor. She became president of her husband's company when he died. The company was Iron Clad Manufacturing Company. At that time, not many women were company presidents. The company made milk cans, barrels, and other steel products. Bly came to hold patents during the early 1900s for several inventions, such as a 55-gallon oil drum and a stackable garbage pail. She also invented an improved milk jar.

Last Years

Eventually, Bly went back to reporting. Later articles were about subjects such as World War II. She was setting records again, this time as America's first woman war reporter. She wrote from the war's front lines. She also fought for the rights of women throughout her life. One way she did this was by writing her own column. She gave advice about different issues. In many ways throughout her life, Nellie Bly found ways to make a difference.

GO ON →

5 Read the sentence from the passage.

She wrote a <u>response</u> to the newspaper, and it was so well-written and interesting that the editor offered Bly a job.

The word <u>response</u> comes from a Latin word that means "to answer." What does <u>response</u> mean?

  A collect

  B deliver

  C avoid

  D reply

6 How did Bly help to solve the problem of bad conditions in different industries?

  A She pretended to work in each industry.

  B She wrote about the conditions so that everyone knew.

  C She entered a race around the world.

  D She became an inventor for her husband's company.

GO ON →

7 Read the sentence from the passage.

When her article was published, the hospital had to make <u>improvements</u>.

The Latin root of <u>improvements</u> means "to use." What word **best** describes what <u>improvements</u> means for the hospital?

A ways of getting faster

B ways to keep things normal

C ways of getting better

D ways to keep things simple

8 Complete the diagram to show what problems Bly faced when she tried to race around the world. Write **two** problems from the box below.

| Bly tries to go around the world in less than 80 days. |

| **Problems** |

Problems

| Bly must take over her husband's business. |
| A snowstorm causes delays. |
| Bly reads an upsetting article. |
| Another reporter is trying to beat Bly. |

GO ON →

9 Read the sentence from the passage.

In her 30s, she decided on a new career by becoming an <u>inventor</u>.

The word <u>inventor</u> comes from a Latin word that means "to come upon, find." What does an <u>inventor</u> do?

A tries

B paints

C sells

D creates

10 How did Bly help women solve different issues they were having?

A by giving advice in the column she wrote

B by using the words of other reporters

C by finding ways to improve steel products

D by becoming the first woman war reporter

Student Name: _____

Question	Correct Answer	Content Focus	Complexity
1	C	Problem and Solution	DOK 2
2	B	Problem and Solution	DOK 2
3	D	Greek and Latin Roots	DOK 1
4	A	Greek and Latin Roots	DOK 1
5	D	Greek and Latin Roots	DOK 1
6	B	Problem and Solution	DOK 2
7	C	Greek and Latin Roots	DOK 1
8	see below	Problem and Solution	DOK 2
9	D	Greek and Latin Roots	DOK 1
10	A	Problem and Solution	DOK 2

Comprehension 1, 2, 6, 8, 10	/10	%
Vocabulary 3, 4, 5, 7, 9	/10	%
Total Progress Monitoring Assessment Score	/20	%

8 Students should complete the diagram with the following problems:
- A snowstorm causes delays.
- Another reporter is trying to beat Bly.

Unit 6 Weeks 1–2 Rationales

1

A is incorrect because finding purple crystals did not solve the problem of being without exploring tools.

B is incorrect because becoming a tour guide for the cave did not solve the problem of being without exploring tools.

C is correct because McDonald solved the problem of having a lack of tools by exploring with candles and string.

D is incorrect because writing about the cave in a journal did not solve the problem of being without exploring tools.

2

A is incorrect because the passage does not state that no one visited the cave when McDonald was away from it.

B is correct because the passage states that McDonald got homesick for the cave and wanted to return whenever he was away from it.

C is incorrect because the passage does not state that McDonald got lost in the cave when he was away from it.

D is incorrect because the passage does not state that no one took care of the cave when McDonald was away from it.

3

A is incorrect because based on the Latin root of *original*, the word does not mean "largest."

B is incorrect because based on the Latin root of *original*, the word does not mean "newest."

C is incorrect because based on the Latin root of *original*, the word does not mean "best."

D is correct because based on the Latin root of *original*, the word means "first."

4

A is correct because based on the Latin root of *studies*, the word means "learning about something."

B is incorrect because based on the Latin root of *studies*, the word does not mean "forgetting about something."

C is incorrect because based on the Latin root of *studies*, the word does not mean "resting the mind."

D is incorrect because based on the Latin root of *studies*, the word does not mean "resting the body."

5

A is incorrect because based on the Latin root of *response*, the word does not mean "collect."

B is incorrect because based on the Latin root of *response*, the word does not mean "deliver."

C is incorrect because based on the Latin root of *response*, the word does not mean "avoid."

D is correct because based on the Latin root of *response*, the word means "reply."

6

A is incorrect because the passage does not state that Bly pretended to work in each industry.

B is correct because the passage explains how Bly reported on the conditions.

C is incorrect because the details about Bly's race around the world have nothing to do with the bad conditions in different industries.

D is incorrect because the details about Bly's involvement in her husband's company are not related to the bad conditions in different industries.

7

A is incorrect because based on the Latin root of *improvements,* the word does not mean "ways of getting faster."

B is incorrect because based on the Latin root of *improvements,* the word does not mean "ways to keep things normal."

C is correct because based on the Latin root of *improvements,* the word means "ways of getting better."

D is incorrect because based on the Latin root of *improvements,* the word does not mean "ways to keep things simple."

8

Students complete the diagram by placing two statements into the "problems" box:

A snowstorm causes delays.

Another reporter is trying to beat Bly.

9

A is incorrect because based on the Latin root of *inventor,* the word does not mean "one who tries."

B is incorrect because based on the Latin root of *inventor,* the word does not mean "one who paints."

C is incorrect because based on the Latin root of *inventor,* the word does not mean "one who sells."

D is correct because based on the Latin root of *inventor,* the word means "one who creates."

10

A is correct because details in the passage explain how Bly gave advice in the column she wrote to help women.

B is incorrect because the details in the passage do not say Bly used words from other reporters.

C is incorrect because the details in the passage do not show how Bly finding ways to improve steel products helped women.

D is incorrect because while Bly does become the first woman war reporter, that detail does not explain how Bly helps women solve different issues they were having.

Read the passage. Then answer the questions.

Jupiter, Neptune, Minerva, and Momus
A retelling of an Aesop Fable (based on an ancient legend)

[*Setting: On Mount Olympus, the home of the gods.*]

NARRATOR: The gods agree to have Momus judge their creations for the world.

JUPITER: Who has made the most wonderful thing? Surely, it is the man I have created.

NEPTUNE: Stop bragging, Jupiter. Momus can see that this bull is best.

MINERVA: No. My house is the grandest creation of all!

NARRATOR: As Momus became jealous and spiteful, he found fault with each.

MOMUS: This bull has a flaw. The horns should be placed below its eyes. That way the bull could see where it is going to strike.

NEPTUNE: What?

MOMUS: And a house without iron wheels is a mistake. How could this house be moved if neighbors prove to be unpleasant?

MINERVA: Wheels on a house?

MOMUS: This man is the worst of all. He should have a window on the outside of his chest so everyone might know his feelings.

JUPITER: [*Becoming angry.*] You find fault with everything we have made, yet you have done nothing good yourself. You cannot comment on the works of others. Leave Mount Olympus at once!

GO ON →

1   What does Jupiter learn in this play?

    A   Minerva is sly and uses tricks to win.

    B   Momus is smart and tries to be useful.

    C   Momus is unhappy and can never be pleased.

    D   Neptune is proud and thinks he is the wisest.

2   Which statement describes a main theme of the play?

    A   Judge fairly or not at all.

    B   Do not attempt the impossible.

    C   It is better to do one right thing.

    D   There is strength in working together.

GO ON →

Read the passage. Then answer the questions.

Mercury and the Woodman

A retelling of an Aesop Fable (based on a Greek story)

[*Setting: A river.*]

MERCURY: What is the trouble here?

WOODCUTTER: [*Staring in disbelief.*] My axe has fallen into the river. I make a living with this tool.

[*Mercury dives into the water and returns with a golden axe.*]

MERCURY: Was this what you had lost?

WOODCUTTER: This is a golden axe. It is not the axe that I lost.

[*Mercury dives into the water and returns with a silver axe.*]

MERCURY: Was this what you had lost?

WOODCUTTER: This is a fine silver axe. It is not the axe that I lost.

[*Mercury dives into the water and returns with a simple axe with a wooden handle.*]

MERCURY: Was this what you had lost?

WOODCUTTER: Yes, that is my axe! I am grateful to you for your kindness.

MERCURY: [*Pleased with the woodcutter's truthfulness.*] As a reward for your honesty, you may keep all three axes as your own.

GO ON →

Progress Monitoring Assessments

3 Read the stage direction from the play.

Staring in <u>disbelief</u>.

What is the root word of <u>disbelief</u>?

A dis

B lief

C bel

D belief

4 Read the stage direction from the play.

Pleased with the woodcutter's <u>truthfulness</u>.

What does the root word of <u>truthfulness</u> mean?

A fact

B fake

C lost

D long

GO ON →

Read the passage. Then answer the questions.

Huginn and Muninn

A retelling of a Norse Myth

[*Setting: A castle where Odin is watching over a grand banquet.*]

ODIN: Where are my ravens? They should be here by now. I worry about Huginn and Muninn. They might not return.

NARRATOR: Huginn and Muninn fly into the hall and sit on either side of Odin.

ODIN: Here you are, my wise friends. How glad I am to see you!

GUEST: [*Whispering to the servant.*] I have those ravens in my garden. They are such ordinary birds. True, their powerful wings lift them into the sky, but is that reason for Odin to keep them near?

SERVANT: They are not common ravens here in Asgard, for Odin has given them special powers. They fly around the entire world and see everything happening. Odin depends on their reports.

HUGINN: There is news. We have seen one of the Frost Giants. He hides by taking the shape of an eagle. He knows we are flying over the ocean and spying, and he doesn't like us around.

MUNINN: He flaps his mighty wings, creating a strong wind so we cannot land. We are forced to perch in thick trees near the shore or be blown away.

ODIN: This cannot be!

HUGINN: It's not a problem. We think of it as a funny game. The eagle eventually gets tired, and then we are free to continue our journey.

GO ON →

ODIN: What did you discover?

MUNINN: The Frost Giants are building settlements on the border. We will keep watching this Frost Giant village to discover why it is being built so close to us.

ODIN: I agree. We must keep track of this situation.

[*Setting: The ocean.*]

NARRATOR: That week, Odin decided to set sail in a ship. He wanted to see the Frost Giant village for himself. He took his ravens with him.

ODIN: My smart and curious ravens, fly high into the sea breeze. We have a long voyage across the open ocean, and we need to know when there is land ahead.

MUNINN: Of course! We will be your guides.

NARRATOR: Hours later, Odin saw the Frost Giant village ahead in the distance, where his ravens were waiting. He was thankful once again for the guidance his faithful friends had given.

GO ON →

5 Draw a line to match **each** word from the play with the meaning of its root.

happening	enjoyment
funny	loyalty
settlements	come to pass
faithful	come to rest

6 How are the ravens important in the play?

A They plan an escape from Odin.

B They keep secrets from Odin.

C They give Odin information.

D They overpower Odin's enemies.

GO ON →

7 Read the sentence from the play.

True, their <u>powerful</u> wings lift them into the sky, but is that reason for Odin to keep them near?

What is the root word of <u>powerful</u>?

A pow

B power

C ow

D ful

8 Which statement describes a main theme of the play?

A Being too clever can lead to trouble.

B No one can escape the future.

C We are all more similar than we think we are.

D The right friends deserve your trust.

GO ON →

9   Read the sentence from the play.

He was thankful once again for the <u>guidance</u> his faithful friends had given.

What does it mean for the ravens to give <u>guidance</u>?

A   move quickly

B   show the way

C   carry things

D   fly up and down

10   What is the main message of the play?

A   Pride leads to downfall.

B   Kindness brings kindness.

C   It helps to have wise friends.

D   Wisdom comes from reading.

Student Name: _____

Question	Correct Answer	Content Focus	Complexity
1	C	Theme	DOK 3
2	A	Theme	DOK 3
3	D	Root Words	DOK 1
4	A	Root Words	DOK 1
5	see below	Root Words	DOK 1
6	C	Theme	DOK 3
7	B	Root Words	DOK 1
8	D	Theme	DOK 3
9	B	Root Words	DOK 1
10	C	Theme	DOK 3

Comprehension 1, 2, 6, 8, 10	/10	%
Vocabulary 3, 4, 5, 7, 9	/10	%
Total Progress Monitoring Assessment Score	/20	%

5   Students should draw lines to make the following matches:
- happening—come to pass
- funny—enjoyment
- settlements—come to rest
- faithful—loyalty

Unit 6 Weeks 3–4 Rationales

1

A is incorrect because Minerva is a wise goddess whose work is condemned by Momus.

B is incorrect because Momus becomes jealous and condemns every work.

C is correct because Jupiter labels Momus as a faultfinder or critic who will never be pleased, and removes him as a judge.

D is incorrect because Neptune, although proud of his work, does not claim to be wisest.

2

A is correct because Jupiter labels Momus as a faultfinder and removes him since he cannot judge fairly.

B is incorrect because the gods do succeed at attempting complex works.

C is incorrect because the meaning is too general; although the gods each believe they've done one right thing, Momus does not succeed as a judge.

D is incorrect because the gods do not work together as they are competing.

3

A is incorrect because dis- is a prefix in *disbelief,* and not the root word.

B is incorrect because *lief* is not the root word of *disbelief.*

C is incorrect because *-bel* is not the root word of *disbelief.*

D is correct because the root word of *truthfulness* is "belief."

4

A is correct because the root word of *truthfulness* is "truth," which means "fact."

B is incorrect because the root word of *truthfulness* does not mean "fake."

C is incorrect because the root word of *truthfulness* does not mean "lost."

D is incorrect because the root word of *truthfulness* does not mean "long."

5

The root word of *happening* is *happen,* which means "come to pass."

The root word of *funny* is *fun,* which means "enjoyment."

The root word of *settlements* is *settle,* which means "come to rest."

The root word of *faithful* is *faith,* which means "loyalty."

6

A is incorrect because the ravens fly out each day and return.

B is incorrect because the ravens reveal to Odin all that they see and hear.

C is correct because the ravens in Norse mythology are helping spirits that whisper all of the news to Odin.

D is incorrect because the ravens take Odin to the Frost Giant village, but they do not overpower any enemies.

Progress Monitoring Assessments

7

A is incorrect because the root word of *powerful* is not *pow*.

B is correct because the root word of *powerful* is *power*.

C is incorrect because the root word of *powerful* is not *ow*.

D is incorrect because *-ful* is the suffix of the word *powerful*; it is not the root word.

8

A is incorrect because the ravens are clever but do not get in trouble for it.

B is incorrect because the play shows Odin trying to figure out the future.

C is incorrect because the ravens are accepted and admired for their differences by Odin.

D is correct because Odin uses the ravens to help him succeed by giving his friends trust.

9

A is incorrect because the root word of *guidance* does not mean "move quickly."

B is correct because the root word of *guidance* is "guide," which means "show the way."

C is incorrect because the root word of *guidance* does not mean "carry things."

D is incorrect because the root word of *guidance* does not mean "fly up and down."

10

A is incorrect because Odin is shown as respected and powerful; he is not experiencing downfall but is guarding against it.

B is incorrect because the connection between Odin and the ravens is one of servitude and represents Odin's intellect rather than his kindness.

C is correct because even though Odin is an intelligent god, he relies on the ravens for gathering additional wisdom.

D is incorrect because the play does not mention anything about Odin gaining wisdom from reading.

Read the poem. Then answer the questions.

My Mom's Brain

Inside my mom's brain
You'll find a thing or two
There's not much fun in there,
Just things for me to do!

5 I want to shoot hoops outside,
I want to play on the court before it rains
"Wait! Hold your horses," she says
She's got chores on her brain.

There's homework to do,
10 And trash to take out,
"Just do it and smile,
Now, don't go and pout!"

At dinner that night there's
Spinach and carrots to eat,
15 "Eat your veggies," she says,
HA! That will be a feat!

I want to watch a movie,
Mom says, "You have to sleep,"
"But there's no school tomorrow!"
20 "Hit the hay now, and not a peep!"

The next day I make my bed,
Straighten my messy room,
I sweep and dust, clean and wipe,
Like a tornado with a broom!

GO ON →

25   I can't read Mom's mind but
After breakfast we take the car
What's in her brain now I wonder
'Cause we are traveling far!

An hour later I understand
30   Mom's brain had hidden a spark,
Friends wait for me at the gate
Of the Great Water Theme Park.

If I drew a map of Mom's brain,
There'd be chores and stuff aplenty,
35   But I'd make room for a special place,
It'd be called "Surprises for Benny!"

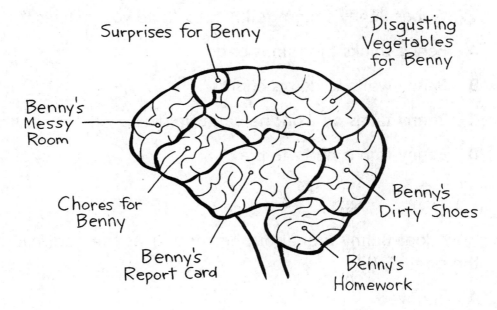

GO ON →

1 By telling mainly about Benny's thoughts, what does the narrator show?

A how Benny is surprised by the special trip

B how his mom chooses the water park

C how Benny invites certain friends to come along

D how his mom wants the chores to be done

2 Read the line from the poem.

"Wait! Hold your horses," she says

Why does Benny's mom tell him to "hold your horses?"

A Benny thinks the rain is bad.

B Benny waits to do his chores.

C Benny takes on work he can't finish.

D Benny is in a hurry to play.

3 How does Benny feel about his mother at the beginning of the poem?

A annoyed

B thrilled

C worried

D uninterested

GO ON →

4   Circle the **two** stanzas that show how Benny feels about his chores.

Inside my mom's brain
You'll find a thing or two
There's not much fun in there,
Just things for me to do!

There's homework to do,
And trash to take out,
"Just do it and smile,
Now, don't go and pout!"

I can't read Mom's mind but
After breakfast we take the car
What's in her brain now I wonder
'Cause we are traveling far!

An hour later I understand
Mom's brain had hidden a spark,
Friends wait for me at the gate
Of the Great Water Theme Park.

5   Read the line from the poem.

"Hit the hay now, and not a peep!"

What does the phrase "hit the hay" mean?

A   run fast

B   go to bed

C   work hard

D   get dressed

Answer Key

Student Name: _____

Question	Correct Answer	Content Focus	Complexity
1	A	Point of View	DOK 3
2	D	Idioms	DOK 2
3	A	Point of View	DOK 2
4	see below	Point of View	DOK 2
5	B	Idioms	DOK 2

Comprehension 1, 3, 4	/6	%
Vocabulary 2, 5	/4	%
Total Progress Monitoring Assessment Score	/10	%

4   Students should circle the first two stanzas.

Unit 6 Week 5 Rationales

1

A is correct because the focus on Benny creates a surprise at the end showing how he isn't aware of his mother's plans.

B is incorrect because Benny's thoughts do not reveal his mother's reasons for choosing the water park.

C is incorrect because it is Benny's mother who invites his friends.

D is incorrect because Benny's mother doesn't comment on why she wants the chores to be done.

2

A is incorrect because Benny doesn't think he's acting in a hurry.

B is incorrect because Benny is doing the opposite of waiting.

C is incorrect because Benny has yet to start his chores.

D is correct because the idiom means "to wait," and although Benny's mother wants him to slow down, he wants to hurry to play.

3

A is correct because the narrator states that Benny just wants to play, and his mother keeps interrupting with chores.

B is incorrect because Benny pouts and argues.

C is incorrect because Benny is frustrated, not worried.

D is incorrect because Benny keeps contemplating what is inside his mother's head.

4

The first two stanzas provide details about Benny's feelings about chores.

5

A is incorrect because the context is that Benny's mother wants him to sleep, not to run fast.

B is correct because the idiom "hit the hay" means "go to bed," and Benny's mother has already told him that he needs to sleep.

C is incorrect because the context is that Benny's mother wants him to sleep, not to work hard.

D is incorrect because Benny's mother wants him to sleep, not to get dressed.